Soccer
The Universal Game

by
Orazio Z. Buttafuoco

DORRANCE PUBLISHING CO., INC.
PITTSBURGH, PENNSYLVANIA 15222

Dedication

*To the memory of
my parents*

Contents

PART THREE

APPENDIX 1

APPENDIX 2

APPENDIX 3

APPENDIX 4

APPENDIX 5 Diagrams:

Acknowledgements

In preparing this book, I have found a tremendous wealth of valuable suggestions and broad assistance. It would have certainly been an impossible task, however, without the cooperation and assistance of the Italian Referees Association's (A.I.A.) world-renown textbook, Casistica, the invaluable bible to all aspiring referees who are lucky enough to pass the severe recruiting selection in order to be admitted to the formal training course which lasts, as it is the case in Italy, about twenty weeks. I also wish to express my deepest personal appreciation to Paolo Biagi, the outstanding Italian journalist, expert on referees matters, who has personally provided me with significant advice and suggestions as well as penetrating criticism. I am also indebted to a dear friend, the late Dr. Benedict Murgarone, and to Dr. Sabino DiGregorio for going over the manuscript, pinpointing, with scholastic analysis, whatever flaws may have emerged or changes which appeared appropriate or needed. I must also express my sincere gratitude to Eddie Pearson, the once supervisor of referees of the NASL (North American Soccer League) who, through his clinics, or indirectly, through his pamphlets, significantly contributed some of the material used in this book interspersely from time to time. And last, but certainly not least, I must express my indebtedness to my wife, Eileen, who has, at all times, been patiently and tirelessly of great stimulus over the years in the preparation of this work.

Preface

The need for a comprehensive treatise on the game of soccer, devised primarily for referees but also for coaches and players as well, has become quite compelling with the rapid progress the game of soccer has achieved of late. The myriad of books, booklets, and pamphlets published over the last decade are geared to a particular need or category of people, seldom or very little to the referees, and only in passing, but quite often to coaches and to players. The present book has been instead prepared with all the protagonists of the game in mind. The many cases presented and analyzed herein {see Part Two, Chapter 4, which is made up of questions (Q) and answers (A)} provide a most valuable assistance to anyone genuinely and actively interested as well as involved in organized soccer. Some of the readers may find a few cases, described in the casebook section (Chapters 7-19), not likely to occur at any one game; however they are discussed with the firm purpose of providing valuable help and a great deal of understanding as well as better comprehension of the rules of the game of soccer. The first chapters—1, 2, and 3—offer a short, descriptive history of the initial phases of soccer development and progress (in particular) in the United States.

This book (knowledge of the basic LAWS OF THE GAME is essential, or at least desirable) should be thoroughly studied by any coaches and players alike if they are to effectively contribute to the increasing success and popularity of the game, but more importantly to understand the decisions of the referees on the field. Constant review of this book is highly recommended: better knowledge, understanding, as well as correct and unequivocal interpretation of the rules of the game make better officials and set a better example.

Introduction

Whenever a game is played, things have a way of going wrong: a player misses a pass by inches or, as often happens, by several yards. All the mistakes made by players never arouse, it seems, the indignation or the furious disapproval of supporting, faithful fans, but only bitterly disappointment if a player has just missed a goal or an easy pass, while the opponents express an obvious sigh of relief if their team has suffered no goal. The situation is reversed if it is the referee that has not detected a foul or has signaled "play-on" after an infraction has occurred. Players and spectators alike seem to find an easy scapegoat and a handy conduit to their frustrations by picking at the twenty-third man on the field, who is only trying to do his job, which far too many are today still unable to comprehend. Large phalanges of soccer fans seem to ignore the fact that the referee is alone on the field and has but about a fraction of a second to judge a foul, whether it is voluntary or not, and then blow the whistle. He has learned that only intentional, deliberate fouls must be called. He has no one to consult but himself. Soccer is unlike any other sport in which you find, normally, at least two referees and as many as six or even seven as we are becoming accustomed to lately, as it is often the case in American football. The referee's job becomes all the more difficult when an individual official involved in a previous match has grossly misinterpreted the rules. Lack of coherent and uniform interpretation and enforcement of the rules of soccer is unacceptable: it is due solely to the clear lack of knowledge and comprehensive understanding of the rules. Reading once or twice the Referee's Chart is obviously never enough; it must be consulted constantly in order first to learn all seventeen laws, to understand them, and finally being able to discuss all the points, which may appear unclear, with other more experienced officials. The proper use of experience and knowledge improves future performances. The practice, though occasionally followed by some Leagues (in the United States) of giving away awards to certain referees for their popularity among managers, should be abandoned forthwith.

A very good referee is not the one seeking on-the-field recognition or approval by outsiders, for the game of soccer is not the kind of setting for a popularity contest. A referee should be judged only by veteran, knowledgeable, and experienced fellow referees, who are the only people who truly understand the pressure and the agonizing decisions he must make at all times and in a split second. A nationwide referee organization has come a long way. Most local referee organizations have only lately begun to run regular, albeit very short, training courses, which are far too inadequate indeed. The practice still common until the late sixties of assigning anyone formally untrained to officially referee a game has had its time. More and more spectators are increasingly jamming playgrounds and stadiums where soccer games are being played; their tastes, refined by observing some outstanding foreign talent, have become vastly more sophisticated. In many American high schools, soccer is replacing other sports, even the almighty American football, for many reasons: it is easier to understand and master, it is open to any size-and-weight individual, and, more significantly, it requires little outlay of money to purchase all the equipment a soccer team needs, which is slightly more than the cost of the massive equipment needed by one or two American football players alone.

Soccer injuries are becoming more infrequent as boys, and now even girls, in high schools and in youth leagues throughout the land acquire more skills. The game of soccer is truly the best conduit to physical fitness. Even prospective athletes taking either American football, or hockey, should play soccer. Soccer practice, with constant ball-kicking, builds the leg muscles and strengthens the ligaments, particularly of the joints. I firmly believe that if any one athlete practiced soccer as a second sport, the likelihood of knee injuries, very frequent in hockey, would be nil. The case that easily comes to mind is the one involving the celebrated super hockey star, Bobby Orr; his many and frequent injuries and surgeries are a sad reminder of an untimely, early end to a spectacular career. It is not presumptuous to state, as many have, that most of the injuries could have seemingly been avoided if Bobby Orr had more extensively practiced, as he had infrequently done, a lot more soccer in the off-season prior to a regular hockey season. Obviously these are pure speculations, but the fact remains that a soccer player has been universally recognized to be the complete athlete.

PART ONE

History of Soccer in the United States

Chapter 1

While doing research about the origin of soccer in the United States, I came about the most astounding and startling answers to some of my questions in the most unlikely source: History of American Football. In it the author (Danzig) retraces all the sports events and activities which eventually led to organized football, American style, as we know it today. It is interesting, certainly enlightening, to learn that as far back as 1820, a game was played by Princeton undergraduates only, "to amuse themselves." They played a ball, football, they called then balloon. At first they used fists to advance the ball, then they began batting it, and later on they just started kicking it. We learn that regular contests were soon organized. A few years later, in 1827, two lower classes at Harvard started the custom of playing each other on the first Monday of the new college year. It was seemingly a crude and rough-played match which inevitably left bruised bodies and torn clothes. At Yale (1840), a rudimentary form of football was being played in which students rushed the football. This primitive form of football was also known, it seems, both at Amherst and Brown. In 1851, Yale freshmen and sophomores organized what was then called a "football rush" for the first time. This practice was discontinued in 1858 when city authorities denied them the use of the city green. During these years, football was played very haphazardly, without rules and without regard to the number of players involved on each side. The game consisted basically of kicking, pushing, slugging, and . . .getting angry. The year 1855 was a significant date, for it was then that round balls made their first appearance. Players began to develop the first rudimentary skills in kicking the ball far and accurately, dribbling and passing. Soccer was beginning to show the first signs of life. In 1860, games began to be played on the Common in Boston, in which a round ball was used between teams representing Boston Latin, Roxbury High, Dorchester High, Boston English, and

short time later, in 1862, the first definite football
nited States was formally formed in Boston when a
Yorker, Gerrit Smith Miller, put together a group of
e was the "Oneida Football of Boston." A monument of
November 21, 1925, at the entrance to the Boston
.., of the club, which, quite interestingly, antedated the
London Football Association.

The date of November 6, or November 13, 1869, according to most sources,
is a very significant one: Princeton played against archrival Rutgers (both
colleges are located near each other). Both colleges presented a set of rules they
had developed independently which were strikingly similar. The game was
played at Rutgers' College Field located at Brunswick, New Jersey. According
to Danzig, the game was a perpetuation of the annual fight between the two
colleges for the possession of an historic cannon that George Washington and
Lord Howe had once struggled for. Princeton put an end to the annual struggle
by sinking the cannon in a bed of solid concrete right on the Princeton campus;
so they played football instead ever since. The game called for twenty-five players
a side. The ball was to be kicked or butted with the head. It suffices to mention
that in December of 1867, a football had been patented by one H. A. Alden
of Matteswan, New York. The bladder was made of rubber and could be
strengthened by canvas. Carrying the ball was forbidden. When the ball was
caught in the air or on the first bounce, the catcher was entitled to a free-kick.
Genuine soccer was, as an infant, taking the first steps. Six goals were necessary
to win a game. (This provision suggests some striking similarities with one of
the rules adopted in recent times in the United States by the North American
Soccer League; this rule has been censored by the FIFA committee, which has
found it unacceptable and contrary to accepted practice by all member nations.)
The goal-posts were twenty-five feet apart. The Rutgers newspaper of the time,
"Targum," reported that the Princeton captain yielded to Rutgers' request to
eliminate free-kicks, whereby the catcher was allowed to boot the ball without
hindrance. During the game, we learn, two players in hot pursuit of the ball ran
into a trail fence which crushed, spilling some of the 200 spectators to the
ground. No uniforms were used, but Rutgers players wore scarlet turbans, while
one wore a scarlet jersey. Rutgers won the game 6 to 4 after scoring the first
goal. As a humorous aside, we may add that one Rutgers player even kicked the
ball into his own goal when he forgot for a moment which way to kick the ball;
this unknown player historically may seemingly be regarded as the first wrong-
way player. It is also interesting to note, as reported by Danzig, that the Rutgers
team won because the players were slimmer and could, quite logically, out-dis-
tance easily the more muscular and slower Princeton players. Also let's point
out that the ball was *round*.

The game in question became the focus of nationwide attention in 1969
when the National Football League celebrated the centennial of American
Football. The reference to the game played in 1869 as a truly American football

4

game was obvious. As described in the foregoing, the history of American football clearly indicates that it was not an American football game that was played in 1869 but actually a true soccer game. It is obvious also that the assumption by the National Football League was quite presumptuous. "Give to Caesar what is Caesar's" is obviously not the policy of the National Football League. The foregoing, I am confident, will and should put the entire matter to rest. The United States Soccer Federation should see to it that justice is rendered by forcefully asserting its rights to a legitimate claim. This is a great country where there is ample room for any one athlete to pursue his or her goal in any chosen sport, including soccer. To the question often raised as to why soccer didn't progress, we gladly suggest an answer by relating a few historical dates and facts, as offered by Danzig himself.

In 1872, the Yale Football Association was organized. Its promoters were strongly influenced by the kind of game, which was essentially soccer, being played by Princeton, Columbia, and Rutgers. The previous year (1871), Harvard had started to play a game, which became known as the Boston game, which clearly resembled rugby. The players used an inflated round ball that could be kicked but, at the same time, it could be picked up at any time and carried. Obviously it was different from the Rutgers game which originally had essentially been a kicking game. The difference between the Harvard game and the Rutgers game was very significant, for had it not been for the fact that Harvard's rules differed so markedly from those of other colleges, the pattern of the American game might have never changed from soccer. In the same year (1871), the Princeton Football Association, the first college football organization of the kind, was organized. Its rules marked the start of organized, codified football. In the fall of 1873, Yale, Columbia, Princeton, and Rutgers sent their representatives to the First Avenue Hotel in New York City where, on October 19, they drew up the first rules and by-laws. Intercollegiate rules in the United States were modeled after the rules of the London Football Association and those of the Princeton and Yale associations. The number of players was limited to twenty. Because of the differences between its rules and those of Princeton and Yale, Harvard declined an invitation to attend the meeting. It is interesting to speculate on what might have been the course of international football in the United States had Harvard accepted to join with the other schools in adopting rules for a game that essentially was soccer. Maverick Harvard definitely was the spoiler and, unknowingly at the time, paved the way for the development of the game that is today as American as the Fourth of July: American football.

In the same year, 1873, Yale played the first intercollegiate and international football game with a team from England, the Eton Players. Yale won 2 to 1 in what must be regarded as the first truly international soccer match played in the United States. Eton fielded eleven players on a side for the first time. At the same time, maverick Harvard continued to play its own brand of game which was basically rugby with a sprinkle of soccer (tokenism!). The following year, 1874, Harvard played three games against McGill University of Montreal, Canada—two of them at Cambridge, Massachusetts, and one at Montreal. Harvard continued to gradually change its game to rugby not only when playing against McGill but also against other colleges as well.

On November 13, 1875, the first game between Harvard and Yale under rugby rules was played at Hamilton Park, Yale campus. Harvard won the match 4 to 0. For the first time, formal uniforms were used in the contest which was witnessed by about two thousand spectators. The new rugby rules began to make considerable headway with other colleges. The following year, 1876, Princeton adopted the new rugby rules under which the Harvard-Yale game had been played the previous year. Other colleges soon joined in. Only one referee was in charge of the game along with two judges representing the two competing teams (see the two club linesmen of present day soccer). The field size was a mammoth 140 x 70 feet. The number of players was set at fifteen. Thus it was essentially rugby rather than soccer that was actually organized into an intercollegiate association in 1876. It was then, from rugby, that the present-day American football eventually evolved, entirely dissimilar in its basic conceptions and structure from soccer, a thing thus truly indigenous to the United States and identified with it only.

Adoption of the game of rugby by Harvard, Princeton, and Yale formed the basis for the present American game, with most of the credit going, inevitably, to Harvard for taking up rugby and for playing it consistently. The number of players on a side was formalized and codified in 1880. The old round ball was discarded and replaced by the egg-shaped leather rugby ball. Training and coaching techniques were developed and applied. The rugby principles of 1876 introduced the novelty of carrying the ball, but the tactics of the times still made the play essentially a kicking game. The rugby-type game became eventually the American game through many evolutionary stages. The transition from soccer was a fait accompli. Thus, conversely, the progress of organized soccer in the United States was painfully slow. While the so-called American national pastime, i.e., baseball, continued to develop and to attract more spectators, particularly at its national final play-off games, presumptuously and erroneously called the World Series (with the entire world totally uninvolved), soccer continued instead to expand and progress throughout the world. No sport played worldwide as soccer can truly and legitimately claim a world championship or series. A soccer world final-round championship series always takes place every four years in a different nation. To its participating sixteen* finalist countries, fourteen** have won qualifying rounds in their zone, with the other two countries representing respectively the present reigning champion and the host

---

*There are now twenty-four (24).
**Twenty-two (22).

country. It suffices here to add that the first World Cup Soccer competition, organized by the international federation, FIFA, occurred in 1930. To the game of soccer belongs the claim for the largest attendance at a single game: 220,000 spectators, at the Maracana Stadium, just outside the City of Rio de Janeiro, Brazil, first used during the World Cup Games in 1950; host Brazil, unfortunately, lost the match to Uruguay for a final score of 2 to 1, leaving the immense crowd quite disappointed, to say the least.

The attendance to soccer matches in the United States dramatically picked up momentum in the 1970s. The largest attendance at a soccer game in North America was first recorded in Montreal, Canada, during the 1976 Olympic games: 71,619, for the final game between Poland and West Germany. More recently a championship game played on August 14, 1977, at the Giants Stadium in East Rutherford, New Jersey, attracted a larger crowd, 77,691 spectators, to watch the acrobatics and the skillful play exhibited by the immortal Péle (duly recognized worldwide as the best soccer player), by Chinaglia and by Beckenbauer, known star performers previously in their respective countries of Brazil, Italy, and West Germany. Among the dignitaries at the game, the distinguished former secretary of state, Doctor Henry Kissinger, a super soccer fan, certainly enjoyed the match and the picture-taking with Péle at the end of the match. Not long afterward, Dr. Kissinger became chairman of the Board of the North American Soccer League.

From the foregoing, one can see clearly how soccer is getting increased attention; the electronic media can no longer ignore a sport that can now attract nearly 80,000 spectators, certainly a hopeful portent.* However massive television coverage of the national pastime continues unabated; ironically on the same afternoon of August 14, 1977, an important baseball game being played only a few miles away at the Yankee Stadium between the local Yankees and the Boston Red Sox was witnessed by only a few thousand spectators. Signs of things to come? The answer is not an easy one. Certainly soccer suffers considerably for lack of adequate exposure, especially on television, where most sportscasters exhibit less than adequate knowledge and understanding of the game. Lack of proper news coverage can be responsible for the modest attendance at local soccer games. There is also much lack of communication and announcement of forthcoming games, at any level, which accounts for the persistent, meager attendance at soccer games. No doubt there is a dire need of educating not only the public but also the members of the press about the aspect of the game of soccer. It is a responsibility that anyone involved with soccer must take, from the leadership of the United States Soccer Federation to anyone at the grass-roots of the soccer spectrum. Everyone must strive for the success of the ever popular sport which has a place, and a legitimate one, on the American sport arena.

---

*The consistent growth of youth leagues in nearly every community nationwide over the last ten years is unmistaken evidence that soccer has become the fastest growing sport in the nation.

A Rule Change

Chapter 2

The recent news of the change by the International Football Association Board to the off-side rule has caught many by surprise, so much so that at first some thought the news to be simply irrelevant indiscretion and little else. For the convenience of the reader, let's take a close look at this change, which is very important and simplifies significantly the rule which, albeit brief, has been the eyesore and torment to every official.

Let's now first recall the complete text of Rule (Law) 11:

A player is off-side if he is nearer his opponent's goal-line than the ball at the moment the ball is played unless:

a. he is in his own half of the field of play;

b. there are two of his opponents nearer to their own goal-line than he is;*

c. the ball last touched an opponent or was last played by him;

d. he receives the ball direct from a goal-kick, a corner-kick, a throw-in, or when it was dropped by the Referee.

Punishment: For an infringement of this Law, an indirect free-kick shall be taken by a player of the opposing team from the place where the infringement occurred.

The rule also makes clear that a player in an off-side position shall not be penalized unless, solely in the opinion of the referee, he is interfering with the play or with an opponent, or is seeking to gain an advantage by being in an off-side position.

The new decision has entirely abolished section C of the Law; henceforth if an opposing player plays the ball last, he doesn't modify the existing position of the player who is in an off-side position.

---

*The two opponents rule (b) no longer applies. If an attacking player is in line with a defending player, there is no off- side.

It seems incomprehensible why Section C of Law 11, which didn't recognize the off-side position of the player after the ball had been played by an opponent, has lasted for so many years. The idea seemingly was to punish an error by a defending player, i.e., a missed clearing kick or a back-pass to the goalkeeper.** It was also meant to be a deterrent against a delaying of the game (see the back-passing to the goalie), but it was also felt by many that Section C was an exceedingly severe penalty and, therefore, one to abolish altogether. Nor must it be forgotten Section C's clear implication which made the situation more confusing: the defending player's mistake nullified the off-side position of the opponent only if he was in a passive off-side (which at present is not punishable). The result was that the poor referee's reflexes were under severe constant pressure, particularly in recent times with the advent of television coverage, which has inexorably and quite frequently exposed the referee to harsh criticism and, in a few isolated cases, to actual assaults by unsportsmanlike, ignorant spectators. This writer has always expressed strong opinion regarding Section C of Law 11, which he personally felt to be excessively vexing. Take, for instance, the case of a defending player who has fallen down and has been unable to avoid the trajectory of the ball and has then been punished by the Law which rectifies the otherwise existing off-side, although a passive one, of the opponent. Thus the elimination of Section C must be favorably and unreservedly accepted, especially at a time when television taping now saves the referee vehement criticism. A case in point is an incident that occurred in Italy not long ago. Soccer devotees still remember, quite vividly, the endless criticism and argument that followed the invalidation by Referee Menicucci (one of the best) of a goal during a first division match (Rome-Milan) which had been scored by Prati (Roma), a serious mistake according to some observers, because a deflection by a defending player (Bet—Milan) had rectified the off-side position of left winger Prati.

It is not the first time that the off-side rule has undergone changes more or less substantial. Let's now look briefly at the evolutionary process and history of the off-side law.

In 1863, the off-side was total; that is when the position of a player was nearer the opponents' goal-line than the ball the moment it was being played forward by a teammate, he was off-side no matter where he was on the field. The first change to the rule just mentioned above was made in 1866 when it was ruled that a player was not off-side as long as he had a least three players anywhere on the field (1) between himself and the opponents' goal-line. The first significant change (to the off-side rule) was made in 1907; it provided that a player was not off-side as long as he was on his own half field; the rest was left unchanged, i.e., the proviso concerning the three opposing players who had to be between the attacking player and the latter's opposing goal-line. Such change to the previous

---

**When a ball is now intentionally passed to the goalie, this "last defender" must kick the ball; he (she) cannot play it with his hands.

stern rule definitely brought about a new tactical game plan; while a team previously assumed the 1-2-3-5 position on the field, with the new off-side rule it became practical for a team's new field position: 1-2-3-2-3, which now saw the two inside forwards take a more back position than the other three forwards (usually the center forward and the two wings). The last substantial change to the off-side rule occurred in 1925. While the off-side position remained as previously stated, i.e., only inside the player's own side of the field, the number of players who had to be between the attacking player and the opponents' goal-line was dropped from three to two. With three players, it was at once easy to have a fullback move forward to quickly put an opponent off-side. The true purpose of the latest change was obviously to stimulate goal scoring, which had considerably decreased with the change made in 1907 (see above). With the off-side to be determined now only if there were less than two players between the attacking player and the opposing goal-line, the defense strategy was affected, for the position of a fullback standing forward was altered: the center halfback now becomes the third fullback who has, as in recent times, developed into the stopper.

The position of the two fullbacks became now clearly anti-wing, while the two inside forwards moved back in support of the halfbacks, a significant tactical change first brought about by Chapman (a well-known British coach).

To conclude this brief disquisition on the off-side rule (and its history), which later became the basis also for a defensive tactical weapon used first by the Hungarians and then by the Latin Americans, let's say that although there are some who disagree with the present format of the off-side rule who have even suggested the outright elimination of the entire Law 11 which, it must be categorically stated, it came into being with the game of soccer, it was included (since its inception) in the first codified set of rules (in 1863) and has never been abolished, only amended with one thing in mind, i.e., to promote international football (not the American version) and the beauty and spectacle of the most popular sport in the world.

The Origin and Definition of Soccer

Chapter 3

The word *soccer* has been in use for several decades now. When the advent of rugby was first recorded in England around the year 1823, a variant to Association football, a confusion of names resulted. After the London Football Association was first formed in 1863 to further the game that emphasized only the kicking of the ball, the game became known as Association football, and through usage of the abbreviation, or of the root, of the word "association" the word "soccer" was coined and adopted.** It derived from soc, i.e., the true root of the word "association"—as—soc—iation—which with the addition of the suffix "er" became "soccer" to indicate the individual playing the game or being associated with the game.

It wasn't until about 1895 that the word soccer seemingly came to be used in the United States to indicate specifically the sport associated with the kicking of the ball.

It is interesting to note that the devotee of the game of soccer came to be known in the United Kingdom originally as "soccerist," a name no longer in usage or even remembered by most.

**See the "Columbia Encyclopedia." Cfr. also the Oxford Dictionary of the English Etymology; also A Comprehensive Etymological Dictionary of the English Language, Vol. 11, by Ernest Klein.

PART TWO

Casebook on the
Laws of the Game

Explanation:

1. Corner flag;
2. Arc of circle of the corner-area: 1.50 m.;
3. Penalty-area: 16.50 m., or 18 yards;
4. Distance of the penalty spot from the goal-line: 9.15 m.;
5. Distance players must observe from the penalty-spot, outside the circle is where opposing players must take position;
6. Radius of a circumference from the center spot in middle field; outside the circle is where opposing players must take position: 9.15 m.;
7. Kick-off spot in the midfield;
8. Halfway line;
9. Optional halfway flag-posts;
10. Corner-area dimension: 1.50 m. from the flag;
11. Penalty-spot;
12. Penalty-area measurement into the field;
13. Goal-area, marked inside the field;
14. Dimension of the goal-area: 5.50 m, or 6 yards;
15. Area outside the perimetral playing field, 1.50 m. wide at least, set aside for players or officials (referee or linesmen only).

The Field of Play (see also diagram 1, Appendix 5, p. 149)

Cases on Law 1
"The Field of Play"

Chapter 4

1. Q. What is meant by the definition:
  a. goal area,
  b. penalty area,
  c. the circle at the center of the playing field,
  d. the corner-area arc of a circle,
  e. the arc of circle outside the penalty area and the use thereof.

  A. a. The goal area is where the ball is placed for the goal-kick. In the same area the goalie cannot be charged if not in possession of the ball, provided he is not obstructing an opponent;
  b. The penalty-area is (the area) where the goalie is allowed to play the ball with his hands, and where the nine infractions—as by law 12—committed by a player of the defending team are punished with a penalty kick. Furthermore it marks the limit the ball must cross on a goal-kick or on a free-kick in favor of the defending team inside the penalty area before it can be replayed. It also marks the zone inside which no opponent can stand on a goal-kick or a free-kick by the defending team. Finally it marks the area outside which all players of both teams must take position on a penalty-kick with the exception of the defending goalie and the penalty kicker;
  c. The circle in the center field marks the minimum distance the players of the defending team must stand on a kick-off;
  d. The corner-area arc-of-a-circle marks the area where, in any spot thereon, the ball is placed on a corner-kick;

e. The arc-of-a-circle outside the penalty-area marks the minimum distance (9.15 meters) all players must keep from the penalty-kick-mark on a penalty-kick.

2. Q. What is the half-way line and its use thereof?

A. It divides into two equal parts the field-of-play and makes it easier for the referee to see that the ball is placed on the right spot and the players are standing on their half of the field on a kick-off and during the game in the event of an off-side. In the latter case, the half-way line belongs to both teams; therefore a player standing on this line must be considered as standing in his own half of the field.

3. Q. If during a match the cross-bar become slightly displaced, it breaks up or completely collapses and it may appear either impossible to repair or replace it, should the match end?

A. Yes. It must be emphasized that the cross-bar cannot be replaced by a rope in order to complete the game.

4. Q. Are the lines marking the boundaries of the field of play and the areas therein also part of the field of play and of the areas within?

A. Yes, insofar as the enforcement of the Laws of the game is concerned.

5. Q. What is the measurement and the shape of the goal-posts as well as the cross-bar?

A. The width and depth of goal-posts and cross-bars cannot be less than 10 cm. nor more than 12 cm. As long as these measurements are followed, the goal-posts and the cross-bars can be square, rectangular, round, semicircular, or elliptical in shape, or as required by the competent association.

6. Q. From which part of the goal-posts must the distance to mark the goal-area and the penalty-area be measured?

A. The distance to mark the goal-area and the penalty-area is to be measured from inside the goal-posts so that the width of the goal-posts will be included in the measurement of both areas.

7. Q. What is the "purpose-field" and its use thereof?

A. The "purpose-field" should be a strict requirement and is a flat area at least 1.50 meters wide next to the perimetral markings of the play-ground. It is of the same nature as the field of play, having the same planimetry and void of any possible material obstruction, ditch, or similar ground formation which could constitute danger to the players. Players can occasionally run into this field-area for a brief time and only for playing reasons, such as: to avoid a checking opponent, to dribble, to avoid an off-side, to take the distance for a throw-in or for a corner-kick.

8. Q. What is the obligation (responsible duty) incumbent upon the referee in matters pertaining to certain measurements to be checked before the match? If one or both teams advance (formal) reservations in what form should they be made in order to be valid?

A. With the exception regarding the size of the ball, which must conform to official regulations and requirements to be checked by the referee— at his own initiative and always before the start of the match—other checks may be made by the referee, whenever he has any doubts regarding certain measurements or if a team has advanced reservations. The latter, which can be made for any reasons concerning any irregularities, must be made in writing and presented to the referee prior to the start of the game. In the event irregularities occur during the match, a team may move reservations (complaints) during the contest and make them oral; in such an eventuality, the referee will acknowledge the reservations (complaints) in the presence of the captain of the other team. If the linesmen are official, it is advisable that at least one of them be a witness to the lodging of any complaints. In the event no gross irregularities are found by the referee, if the measurements comply with the minimum or maximum requirements set forth by the competent association, the game shall begin. The referee will indicate in his report any discrepancies he has verified, otherwise he will compel (mandate) the home team to correct the irregularities and, upon refusal, he will not start the game.

9. Q. Can a game be played on a field covered with snow?

A. Yes, provided there is no danger to the players. The field must, in this case, be marked with powdered charcoal or similar material.

10. Q. At what precise time must the referee give his final decision on the impracticability—or other causes—of the field of play which may interfere with the normal conduct of the match?

A. Any final decision on the impracticability of the field of play rests solely with the referee assigned to the game. He will first proceed to the identification of the players, and then will examine the playground in the presence of the two captains at the time the game is scheduled to start or before if both teams are already on the field of play.

11. Q. Can the referee refuse to start a game if the goals have no nets?

A. Except when provided otherwise, nets are to be mandatory; lacking them, the referee shall not start the game.

12. Q. Can a game continue to be played if, during its progress, the field-markings become invisible?

A. As soon as a considerable portion of a marking—or the most significant one—has faded away, the referee must immediately stop the match and summon the captain of the home team requesting that the lines be re-marked and made clearly visible again before resuming play. Whenever it appears virtually impossible to re-mark the field, the referee must suspend the match for good; the reasons for the suspension of the game must be described in full details in his report.

13. Q. If a game has started, when should the referee call it off for lack of visibility?

A. The final decision is up only to the referee. He must at all times have full view of the entire field of play and of both goals. As a rule, the referee determines there is sufficient visibility if he can see one goal from another. In international matches, visibility is ascertained by standing in the middle (center) of the field. In any case, the referee can proceed to ascertain whether there is sufficient visibility upon request—always legitimate (justified)—by any one of the two captains.

14. Q. Can a game, begun in daylight, be completed with artificial lighting?

A. Unless provided otherwise by the competent local association and for specific games, there is no reason why a game cannot be continued and completed with artificial lighting. However, if during a game visibility becomes inadequate because of sudden appearance of fog or unforeseen early darkness, the match must be immediately ended.

15. Q. Can a game be ended because of strong winds?

A. Yes. The referee must call off the game, even temporarily, when because of strong and persistent winds the ball cannot remain stationary on the field upon resumption of play. The game will be called off for good whenever the wind persists in its violence or even increases its intensity, thus making it impossible to continue playing.

16. Q. If the corner-flags—or the linesmen's flags—do not conform with the required color (preferably yellow), what should the referee do?

A. The referee should invite the home team—through the captain—to substitute the faulty flags. Whenever such replacement becomes an impossibility, the referee shall begin or continue the game, but he must nonetheless report all the facts to the competent authorities.

17. Q. Is it necessary to place two flags opposite the half-way line on each side of the field of play, not less than 1 meter outside the touch-line?

A. No, but it is desirable.

18. Q. Is it a requirement that the corner-flag posts be not less than 5 feet (1.50 meters) high? If they were higher than 1.50 meters, would they be considered regular?

A. As long as they are a minimum of 5 feet (1.50 meter) high, flag-posts can be higher, for no rule sets forth a precise measurement other than the minimum. In any case, the referee has the sole discretionary powers to accept or reject any flag-posts which, to his judgment, appear very dangerous and whose functional height is improper.

Cases on Law 2
"The Ball"

Chapter 5

1. Q. If a game is played on a neutral field, which club should supply the ball(s)?

    A. Normally both clubs should each supply at least two balls which meet the requirements set forth in Law 2. The referee shall always choose the ball to start the game, if argument rises over the conditions of any one ball.

2. Q. Does the exclusive right to select the ball to start the game belong to the referee?

    A. The law compels the referee to examine the ball(s) and make sure they all meet the requirements as by Law 2, but does not necessarily choose the one to start the game. It is strongly advisable that the referee abstain from taking such an initiative. (The ball to be used should be the one supplied by the home club.) If a controversy arises over the condition of the ball supplied by the home club, the referee must intervene and choose the ball. A match must be started and finished, whenever possible, with the same ball. No substitution should be made unless the referee detects sudden imperfections. The ball can, however, be replaced temporarily, for the sake of saving time, with another ball to be examined by the referee, if he has not already done so.

3. Q. If only one ball is available before the game, should the referee start the game?

    A. Yes. The availability of extra balls is advisable only in order to complete the game which otherwise would be impossible if the original, single ball has become deflated in the course of a match.

4. Q. If the ball becomes suddenly irregular during the game—it bursts or becomes deflated—what should be done?

A. As soon as the referee detects the imperfection, he must at once stop the play and resume it by dropping the new ball on the precise spot where the irregular ball was when the play was interrupted. If the ball bursts at the precise moment it is kicked but goes into the goal, the goal must be disallowed.

5. Q. During a kick-off or a resumption of play—free-kick, goal-kick, corner-kick, penalty-kick, throw-in—if the trajectory of the ball is interrupted by a spectator or by any strange obstacle, what decision should be taken?

A. The referee must resume play by dropping the ball on the precise spot where the interference occurred, except in the case of a penalty-kick, which must be retaken.

6. Q. If during the intermission or when kicked outside the field of play the ball ends in the water—puddle or bucket—what decision is required, particularly if a complaint is lodged by the opposing team?

A. First of all the ball should never be subject to alterations or treatment leading to structural alteration of same. Thus whenever such condition occurs the referee shall replace the damaged ball with another in perfect condition. If the alteration has been caused by a player, he shall be cautioned; otherwise the incident should be reported, by the referee and/or by any other game official.

7. Q. If the officially approved ball becomes defective during the game, what should be done?

A. Provided the irregularities do not affect the circumference or weight of the ball, as long as the new apparent irregularity does not affect the circumference or appear dangerous to the players and the ball basically reflects the fundamental characteristics as at the time of the kick-off, the ball should not be replaced. If all the available balls, previously checked and accepted by the referee, become gradually defective, the referee shall closely observe the behavior of both teams in such circumstances. Whenever he detects deliberate, reckless behavior and demeanor, and whenever no other perfect ball is offered to the referee, he shall call the game off and report the incident.

Cases on Law 3
"Number of Players"

Chapter 6

1. Q. How relevant are the line-ups of the teams which are handed to the referee before a game?

   A. They are extremely relevant, for they allow players to play the game and to be identified quickly by the numbers appearing on the jersey they are wearing, which must correspond to those appearing on the official line-up.

2. Q. In an official match, if the teams show up without officially approved pass-cards (identification cards), should the referee start the match?

   A. The players participate in official games only if in possession of the pass-cards issued by the competent league or association. The referee can waive such rule as long as the club official in charge of the team can state (in writing, i.e., taking full responsibility also extended to the club) that a player (or players) without a pass-card is duly registered with the association under whose jurisdiction the game is being played, and that the club has requested, not later than a day preceding the match, that the player (or players) be issued valid pass-cards. In such a case, the players must be identified by official documents, such as driving license, immigration-alien card, etc., issued by government agencies or other sports organizations provided they bear a photograph.

3. Q. Is it required that a team have a captain?

   A. The answer is unequivocally yes. The referee must make sure throughout the game that captains of both teams be present at all times as required. Furthermore the referee should make sure that a player acting as captain be identified on the official line-up; a co-captain can also be required to be identified so that he can duly substitute that captain if the latter becomes incapacitated during the course of the match.

4. Q. At the official kick-off time, only one team is present. How long should the referee wait for the other team?

A. Except as provided otherwise, the referee should wait a maximum of forty-five minutes from the officially scheduled kick-off time. It is forbidden for the assigned referee or for other referees present at the match to officiate the game subsequently as a friendly match. The official starting time is when the referee and the players are inside the playground in their respective uniforms ready to start the game. In any case, the referee must, well before the official time, proceed to the identification of the players already present on the field, requesting the line-ups (2), even though the game may not get underway, except when the playground is not in playing condition.

5. Q. If at the time of the official kick-off the playground is being used by two other teams playing an official game, what should be done?

A. In such a case the game shall begin as soon as the playground becomes available. No waiting time is required from the end of the preceding match in case a team is late.

6. Q. At the call of the referee (the moment he blows the whistle) the captain of one of the teams requests the referee to delay the kick-off until other late players arrive. Is such a request in order?

A. Yes. The referee shall by the rules wait for a maximum of forty-five minutes in order to start the game, except as provided otherwise by the competent league or association. However if a team shows up with at least seven players, the referee shall immediately begin the game.

7. Q. Whenever, because of extenuating circumstances of which the referee has been timely made aware of, a team cannot reach the playground within the prescribed period of forty-five minutes from the scheduled starting time, is the referee under obligation to wait still further?

A. Final judge of exceptional or extenuating circumstances is the competent league or association. The referee, in any case, cannot waive the rule which unequivocally spells out the obligation by the referee to wait the prescribed forty-five minutes from the official kick-off time, except where specific guidelines have been set forth by the competent league or association because of technical or organizational needs.

8. Q. Once it is ascertained a team is late, is it necessary that the referee wait on the field of play?

A. No, it is not. The referee should retire to his dressrooms and wait there.

9. Q. If a team shows up late and, more specifically, at about the end of the prescribed forty-five minutes waiting period with its players not yet in uniforms (or playing attire), should the game be played?

A. The game should start at the latest at the expiration of the forty-five minutes waiting period. However, if the referee has proceeded to the identification of the players (of the late team) just prior to the expiration of the forty-five minutes waiting period, the game can begin as soon as the players have worn their uniforms, in the shortest possible time.

10. Q. A team begins the game with less than eleven players. When can late players join their team while the game is underway?

A. In order to start a match, the players on the field must number at least seven per team. If the late players have been identified by the referee right before the start of the game, they can enter the playground while the game is in progress, provided they have received permission from the referee to enter the field. The late players not identified prior to the start of the game can enter the playground only during the brief stoppages of the game. They must go to the referee and be properly identified.

11. Q. If a late player does not behave according to the rules outlined above (10), what action should be taken?

A. Except where the enforcement of the advantage rule applies, the careless player should be cautioned and the play, if interrupted because of the player's demeanor, must be resumed with an indirect free kick from the spot where the player first entered the playground. If the same player is guilty of more serious offense, he should be punished according to Rule 12.

12. Q. If a late player, already in uniform who has not reported to the referee to be identified, stands outside the sidelines, the goal-lines, or even inside the playground, intentionally hits an opponent player who is participating in the match and while the ball is in pay, what action should the referee take?

A. As soon as the referee ascertains the facts, he shall stop the play, shall identify the player, and then shall eject him from the game. Since the foul was committed within the playing field, a direct free kick shall be assessed. If the infraction occurred inside the penalty area, a penalty-kick shall be awarded.

13. Q. If during a match the number of players in a team is reduced to less than seven because of injuries or other causes, but not because of disciplinary actions, should the game be suspended?

A. Whenever the referee realizes that the injuries are not serious and anticipates the quick re-entry of the injured player, he shall suspend the match temporarily, notifying the two captains of his intentions of resuming the play very shortly.

14. Q. Can a goalie be replaced by another player on the field during a match without first notifying the referee?

A. No. Once the game has started, the goalie can be substituted by another player already on the field or the reserve goalie only after the referee has been notified. This rule is in force for the duration of the game, including the sporadic interruptions and the interval.

15. Q. Can a player be substituted during official matches?

A. Yes, but only by substitutes whose names appear on the lineup. The competent league or association can, in certain tournaments, authorize the use of other substitutes by issuing specific rules which outline the procedure in such contingencies. Furthermore two clubs can substitute players during friendly matches, provided an agreement has been reached in advance by the two clubs.

16. Q. A substitute player, in the absence of a linesman, is utilized in such duty by the referee. Can such player subsequently substitute a player and leave the duty of linesman to someone else?

A. No. The player performing the duties of a linesman cannot participate in the match as a player.

17. Q. A player leaves the field of play during the game—not because of injuries—without the referee's permission and then re-enters the field while the play is in progress. What action should the referee take?

A. Except where the advantage rule is applicable, the referee shall stop the play, shall caution the player, and shall award an indirect free-kick in the exact spot where the infraction occurred. If the play has not been interrupted, the referee shall caution the player as soon as the first interruption of play occurs.

18. Q. A player leaves the field of play without the referee's permission but only because of tactical reasons connected with the play. Should he be dealt with by the referee?

A. No.

19. Q. A player leaves the playground during the game, not because of injuries, without the referee's permission, and does not come back. What action should be taken?

A. The referee shall deem the action as misconduct and report a caution to the competent authority—league or association since he could not notify the caution directly to the player.

20. Q. What should the referee do if during a match he suddenly notes that there are twelve players in a team?

A. The referee shall stop the play immediately, since the extra player must be considered an unauthorized person, then he will ascertain, based on the available pass-cards in his possession, who the intruder is so that he can report the incident to the competent league or association; he shall then invite the intruder to leave the field immediately. If the twelfth player, or individual, is one of the substitutes whose name appears on the lineup, he shall be ejected from the game. (The referee shall request the captain to assist him.) The play shall be resumed by the referee by dropping the ball on the spot where it was at the time the play was stopped.

Cases on Law 4
"Players' Equipment"

Chapter 7

1. Q. At the beginning or during the course of a match, should players be allowed to play without jersey and shorts?

A. Normally players are not allowed into the playground without jersey or shorts. If during the match players should end up without jerseys or shorts, the referee shall invite the players to leave the field at once and adjust, or complete, their equipment but without interrupting the play even temporarily and allowing them to join their team on the field without requesting his (the referee's) permission, unless the number of players has dropped to less than seven. If, because of unusual circumstances, the players cannot outfit themselves with the required equipment, the referee shall allow them to resume their participation in the match, as long as they are wearing items which are acceptable and do not offend morality and do not constitute danger to other players and, in any case, do not cause difficulty to the normal function of officiating.

2. Q. Whenever, before the kick-off or later during the match, two players of the same team wear the same number on their jerseys, what action should be taken?

A. The referee shall request that one of the players wear no number at all and make the necessary annotations.

3. Q. Can a player change the numbered jersey during a game?

A. If the players' numbers appear on the line-up handed to the referee before the kick-off, the jersey's substitution shall not be allowed, except when a goalie requests replacement with another player already on the field (one of the eleven players). If the exchange of jerseys occurs without first informing the referee, the latter shall stop the play as soon as he detects the infraction and shall invite the two players to resume the original attire which will show the original numbers identifying the players as by the line-up. The referee shall then caution the two players and resume the play by awarding an indirect free-kick against the player guilty of having exchanged the numbered jersey.

4. Q. Can a player participate in a match without shoes (booths)?

   A. No. Once a player is found wearing only one shoe (booth) or none at all, the referee shall stop the play, unless he intends to apply the advantage rule, and shall invite the player to leave the field and return with proper shoes (booths). If the player is unable to find any shoes (booths), he shall not be allowed to participate in the match. The play, if interrupted for such reason, shall be restarted by the referee, who will drop the ball on the spot where it was when the play was stopped.

5. Q. What procedure should a player follow when leaving the field to adjust his equipment?

   A. He can re-enter the field when the ball is not in play (or the play has stopped) and report to the referee who will then make sure the equipment is in order. If the player has been sent off the field to adjust his equipment and re-enters while the play is in progress and the play is then stopped, the referee shall caution the player and award an indirect free-kick from the spot where the guilty player was (when he re-entered).

6. Q. Can a player participate in a match with regular (daily) shoes instead of prescribed booths?

   A. The rule (4) does not specify that a player must wear a particular type of shoes or booths. However if the regular shoes appear equipped with bars or studs, these must then conform to the standard set forth by the rule (4).

7. Q. Can a player participate in a match wearing glasses?

   A. Yes. He cannot, however, wear wristwatches, metal bracelets, or other objects which may cause injury to other players.

8. Q. While the game is in progress, the referee notices a player wearing objects not permitted by the law (4). What action should he take?

   A. Whenever the referee perceives the willingness (clear intention) of hiding dangerous objects such as wristwatches, rings, metal bracelets, etc., he shall request the player to do away with any of them. If, on the other hand, the player refuses to abide by the referee's ruling, he shall be ejected from the field. If, in the referee's opinion, a player intentionally hides dangerous objects, he shall be ejected from the game.

9. Q. If a player with a previous injury appears on the field wearing a cast—even as a protective measure to avoid further injuries—should the referee decide before the kick-off that the cast or any form of bandage constitute a potential danger to other players?

A. Yes. If the referee sees that the bandage, or cast, can constitute a potential danger to other players, he shall prohibit the player from taking part in the game.

Casebook on Law 5
"Referees"

Chapter 8

1. Q. The referee assigned to officiate a match arrives on the field and finds that the game has already started with another referee officiating. What should he do?

   A. He shall not interfere with the proceedings, but he shall report everything in detail to the competent league or association.

2. Q. Can a referee assigned to officiate a game of higher division request the stoppage of a match of lower division if, in his opinion, the continuation of the other game could prejudice the conditions of the playground and render it not entirely feasible for the more important match?

   A. No, unless ruled otherwise by the competent league or association.

3. Q. If a referee cannot complete officiating a game for any reason, can he be substituted by another referee present on the field?

   A. No. An assigned referee cannot be substituted after a game has started nor can it be continued as a friendly match.

4. Q. When should a referee suspend a game because of field conditions?

   A. When the field is flooded or there is danger to the welfare of players. A temporary suspension is ruled by the referee if he foresees that conditions can change, otherwise he shall call the game off. After an interruption (rainshowers, etc.), the referee shall summon the two teams into the field and resume the play. In the above described cases, the referee shall:
   1. record exactly the time when the interruption occurred;
   2. note where the ball was at the time the interruption occurred;

3. notify the two teams (captains) and the linesmen, if they are official (neutral), that the teams must remain on a standby basis and at his disposal until ruled otherwise.

5. Q. If the referee has ruled that a match cannot be played (because of field conditions or other reasons), or after calling a game off already underway (following a temporary suspension), can he accept to officiate the same match as a friendly game?

A. No. Neither the assigned referee nor neutral assigned linesmen nor other referees present on the field can officiate the game as a friendly match.

6. Q. What shall a referee do if his watch breaks down?

A. He must go to the linesmen, if they are neutral. Whenever both neutral linesmen agree on the time, the referee shall comply with their stand, otherwise he shall call the game off. To offset such (an) eventuality, the referee should always come to the game with two watches (at least one should be a stopwatch) in perfect functioning conditions.

7. Q. From what time and until what time are players under the referee's jurisdiction?

A. As far as enforcement of the technical regulations of play is concerned, the time begins technically with the kick-off and ends at the closing of the game. As far as disciplinary ruling is concerned, the referee's power begins at the time he enters the field (playground), dressrooms, etc., to caution guilty players or to prohibit them from participating in the match. Upon a team's request, the referee shall allow a player not allowed to play to be substituted by another properly registered player (and with a pass-card) whose name must appear on the line-up, provided the above condition occurs prior to the kick-off. If, for instance, two players get involved in a fist fight in the field prior to the kick-off, the referee shall eject the two players from the game and shall allow their substitution. The incident must be reported in detail to the competent league or association. A substitute player ejected before or after the start of the match cannot be replaced. If the same incident occurs after the start of the game, the referee shall eject the two players from the game and shall allow no substitution.

8. Q. What does advantage rule mean?

A. It means that the referee must not intervene to punish any infringement of rules if, in his opinion, his intervention and subsequent stoppage of play would be of advantage to the team to be punished. In any case, although not stopping the play at the time of the infraction, the referee must whenever necessary punish the guilty player at the first suspension of play. Such rule applies, generally, in any situation which requires the referee's intervention. In any case, once the referee allows the play to continue, he cannot technically alter his stand even though the effect of his decision (to let the play continue) didn't produce anticipated outcome (even the score of a goal). The enforcement of the advantage rule is justified only when it is evident and timely.

9. Q. If a team engages in obstructionism, what should the referee do?

A. In the case of far-too-evident and intentional time-wasting tactics and persistent disregard of refraining from such behavior, the referee shall caution the captain and if he shows solidarity with his players he shall be ejected from the game. Should the substitute captain (co-captain) be unable to bring order among his teammates, the referee shall call the game off and report the incident to the competent league or association. If the captain cooperates instead and is sincere in his efforts, albeit unsuccessful, the referee shall impose no disciplinary sanctions on the captain but shall call the game off (before time). Only in exceptional circumstances whenever the potential for incidents by the spectators or by the players appears evident, the referee (in apprehension for his welfare) may allow the game to continue pro-forma, and the incidents must be exactly reported in detail to the competent league or association.

10. Q. The two captains agree to give up the interval allowed by rule, but one of the players demands that he will make use of the allotted interval. What should the referee do?

A. Players have the right to an interval allowed by the rule, and the referee is required to enforce such right.

11. Q. Can the captain of a team eject a teammate from the playground for having committed a certain misconduct?

A. No. Only the referee can eject a player. A player sent off the field by his own captain cannot be regarded by the referee as ejected from the game; thus the player can at any time re-enter the field of play as long as he abides by the rule (how and when he can re-enter the field of play).

12. Q. Whenever a team, as a protest or for other reasons, refuses to continue playing after the game has started, what should the referee do?

A. The referee shall consider the game terminated even though the team that left the field decided subsequently to return to the field and resume play. The referee cannot change his previous decision. The incident must be reported in full detail to the competent league and association.

13. Q. Whenever serious facts occur, such as collective insubordination (by players, etc.), threatening behavior by the spectators, etc., and the referee realizes that by suspending the game he would exasperate further everybody and cause a possible riot dangerous to his and to the players' welfare, can he continue to play the game?

A. Whenever every means employed to keep the game under full control has appeared ineffective, the referee shall, in order to avoid the worse, continue to officiate the match pro-forma and shall note the exact time the game normally played ended, describing in his report, in details, all the circumstances which forced him to officiate the game in an abnormal fashion without full respect of all the rules and regulations of the game. The referee shall inform, at the right time and in the best of circumstances, the linesmen, if neutral, of his decision and the reasons for continuing to play the match. While it rests in the power of the referee to call a game off on account of episodes which he finds harmful to the safety of the players and of himself, the final decision as far as the final score is concerned rests solely with the competent league or association (disciplinary committee).

14. Q. The referee whistles the end of the first half but the linesmen point out to him, or he himself realizes suddenly, that there are still a few more minutes left to play: the referee realizes he made a misjudgment. What shall he do? What if the referee realizes he made an error only during the interval?

A. The referee shall at once summon the players into the field, resume the play in the prescribed form (when it ended) and complete the first half. Subsequently he shall allow the players to enjoy the required interval, even though the players were already enjoying their rest (note second part of question).

15. Q. If the referee prematurely calls the end of the game at the end of the half, what shall he do?

A. If the players are still on the field of play, in the immediate vicinity (adjacent to the field) or already in the dressrooms, the referee shall summon them to the field and resume play to complete the match, unless one or more players are already showering themselves. Any refusal by the players to resume play shall be recorded by the referee and fully reported.

16. Q. Can the referee accept comments or request of information by the players?

A. The referee must never allow comments or requests for information be made to him by any of the players (only the captains can address the referee even though to inquire for anything or to make remarks). The player guilty of such acts shall be cautioned and, if he persists in the same behavior, he shall be ejected from the game. The captain shall be the only one to address the referee with due respect and only when the play has stopped, and only to inquire about a decision. The referee shall never inform anyone about the time left to the end of the period. Any infringement of this law shall be deemed by the referee as misconduct. Thus if the play has been suspended it shall be restarted by an indirect free-kick against the team of the player guilty of the infringement from the spot where the infraction occurred. It is required of the captain as well as of the players never to address the linesmen.

17. Q. A player has been ejected from the game; while he is on his way to the dressroom, a linesman (neutral) informs the referee that the player ejected was not the guilty one. What shall the referee do?

A. If the referee realizes he has made a mistake and while the play has not resumed, he shall recall the ejected player into the field and at the same time eject the guilty player. If, however, the play has resumed, the referee shall not change his decision but shall report all the facts to the competent league or association.

18. Q. Right after the start of the first period, the referee realizes that the team that had chosen the side (of the playground) has also taken the kick-off. Can the referee stop the game and start all over again?

A. If only a few moments have elapsed from the erroneous kick-off or no significant play has developed on the field, the referee shall restart the game ex novo, otherwise he shall let the play continue. In any case, he shall report the incident. Similar procedure should be followed whenever an erroneous kick-off occurs at the start of the second half.

19. Q. What should a referee do if he sees a player lighting a cigarette during the game?

A. The referee should caution the player guilty of misconduct.

20. Q. What should a referee do if a player ejected from the game refuses to leave the field?

A. The referee shall request the captain to enforce his ruling, but if the captain instead takes the player's side, he shall also be ejected from the game and the referee shall request the co-captain to cooperate. If the latter refuses to obey and support the referee, the latter shall whistle the end of the match and shall report the incident in full detail to the competent league or association.

21. Q. A forward player falls down inside the opposing penalty-area without being fouled and does not get up. The referee lets the play continue inside the penalty-area believing the injury was not serious. The play continues inside the penalty-area and the player still on the ground is not only in danger himself but his presence impedes the play to continue smoothly. What should the referee do?

A. The referee shall immediately stop the play, have the injured player transported outside the field of play and quickly resume playing by dropping the ball on the spot where it was when the play was stopped.

22. Q. A player gets hurt accidentally or becomes ill. What should the referee do?

A. The referee shall stop the play and shall have the injured player transported outside the field of play. The play shall then be resumed with the referee dropping the ball on the spot where it was when the play was stopped. In the case of a very serious injury it is suggested to consult a doctor before allowing the injured player to be removed. The incident should be reported.

23. Q. A team is late re-entering the field after the interval despite repeated calls by the referee. What action should be taken?

A. If the referee, after returning to the filed following the interval notices the absence of one of the two teams, he must distinctly summon the other team (using the whistle), waiting briefly for their arrival. If the team persists in not showing up, the referee must check into the dressrooms and notify the captain of the late team regarding their unjustified absence from the field. If the captain clearly shows to be ready to resume play along with at least six other players the referee shall again summon the team to re-enter the field and then resume the second half immediately (with the minimum of seven players). If, however, the captain shows intentions quite evident of not playing the second half, the referee shall request, whenever possible, a written statement on the matter and shall call the game off for good.

24. Q. A person, or an animal, enters into the field or a strange object is thrown into the field during the play; what action should the referee take?

A. When a person or other strange bodies or objects (reserve balls, animals, objects of different nature, etc.) end up inside the field, the referee shall stop the play at the most opportune instant and resume it by dropping the ball on the spot where it was at the time the play was stopped, but after the field has been cleared of the person(s) or object(s).

25. Q. Following a hard shot, the goalie that has intercepted the ball, but cannot avoid that the same end up in goal, remains on the ground visibly and seriously hurt and thus unable to make any moves to stop the ball and avoid the goal. What action should the referee take?

A. The referee shall stop the play and summon assistance for the injured goalie. If the ball, after the interception by the goalie and before the stoppage of the play has crossed the goal-line, the referee shall award a goal. Otherwise he will resume the play by dropping the ball on the spot where it was at the time the play was stopped.

26. Q. A linesman signals that the ball has crossed a side-line, but before the referee sees the signal a defensive player strikes an opposing forward inside the former's penalty-area. What should the referee do?

A. The referee must first administer his disciplinary decision and then resume the play with a throw-in, because the ball was already out when the foul occurred.

27. Q. What instructions should the referee give to the linesmen?

A. The referee shall conform to what is prescribed by the Rule (6) and by what is outlined in any one of booklets available on "...cooperation between referee and linesmen." (See also Chapter 23, Part Three, p. 97.)

28. Q. If the ball goes into goal after striking the face of the referee who, at the time, is unable to observe the proceeding, can the goal be awarded?

A. Yes, but only upon a ruling by an appointed (neutral) linesman that a goal has been properly scored.

---

*See Chapter 23, Part Three.

Cases on Law 6
"Linesmen"*

Chapter 9

1. Q. What instructions are given to the linesmen?

   A. The linesmen must conform strictly to the instructions given by the referee. In case of objections given by the teams, the neutral linesmen must avoid at all times to supply opinions or decisions, unless the referee expressly requests them to do so; in such case, the linesman's opinion becomes binding upon the referee. (See Chapter 24, p. 99.)

2. Q. Can the referee request the opinion of a neutral linesman to ascertain if a ball has entirely crossed the goal-line between the goal-posts?

   A. Yes.

3. Q. Besides the referee, can neutral linesmen disclose to the players, club officials, or other persons authorized by the referee to stand near the touch lines, the time elapsed, or the time left to the end of the match?

   A. No. Under no circumstances should linesmen supply information to anyone about the time left to play; the information, if ever supplied, could very possibly conflict with the opinion of the referee who is the only judge and timekeeper of the game.

4. Q. Can a linesman call the referee's attention to an incident or a serious misconduct the referee didn't detect? What action should the referee take?

---

*See Chapter 24, Part Three.

A. In the case of violent conduct (to strike or attempt to strike an opponent) or serious foul play (to insult, to spit at another player or any official, etc.) by a player toward other players or a neutral linesman, the latter will call the referee's attention by waving the flag. Whenever the referee is unable to notice the signal, the other linesman must repeat the same signal given by the colleague until the referee has detected it. If the referee is still unable to notice the second signal, a quite unlikely possibility, the linesman standing closer must, at the first stoppage of play, enter the field of play and notify the referee of the incident. In either case, the referee shall eject the guilty player from the game. If the linesman's signal is immediately detected by the referee and the infraction has occurred inside the field of play and while the play is in progress, the referee shall stop the play and shall take the required disciplinary action (ejection from the game) as well as the technical action as required: (1) direct free-kick, or penalty-kick whenever violent conducts was committed; (2) indirect free-kick whenever violent behavior against a linesman was committed (if inside the playground), or for serious foul play towards anyone.

In case the linesman is unable to inform the referee until during the interval about incidents which occurred during the first half or at the end of the game, inside or outside the confines of the playground, the referee shall summon in his dressroom the captain of the team of which the guilty player is a member and will inform him of his decision to eject the guilty player from the game.

In any case, the linesman is required to file a report at the end of the game regarding the incident, to which the referee shall attach his own report in which he also shall describe the same incident.

5. Q. Can a referee start a game with only one linesman?

A. No.

6. Q. For any reason whatever, a linesman forfeits his assigned duties without the referee's knowledge, should the game be continued?

A. For the duration of the game two linesmen are required. Therefore, as soon as the referee notices the absence of one linesman, he shall replace him with another. The referee shall report the incident and the precise minute it occurred.

7. Q. At games of lower divisions to which no official (neutral) linesmen have been assigned, can the referee replace the club-assigned linesmen with two colleagues present at the game?

A. No.

8. Q. Whenever one or both neutral linesmen are unable for any reason to continue fulfilling their duties, what should the referee do in such contingency?

A. The referee shall substitute the linesman, or both, with another (or both) neutral one(s) whenever possible, or with two registered players the two clubs have in their rosters. Once the substitution has been made it is final.

Cases on Law 7
"Duration of the Game"

Chapter 10

1. Q. When does the game actually start, at the whistle of the referee, or when the ball is actually played (kick-off) as far as computation of time is concerned?

   A. The time must be computed from the moment the play has regularly started.

2. Q. Must there be allowance for time lost?

   A. The referee shall record all lost time and make allowance for it at the end of each period. Time lost during the first half cannot be added to the normal duration of the second half.

3. Q. How should lost time be computed?

   A. Since the duration of the game shall have two equal periods of forty-five minutes (total 90 minutes), the referee must record any interruptions of play which may occur for any cause lasting at least one minute, disregarding fractions of seconds, and adding them to the normal duration of each period (as explained above). Deliberate delays of the game, due to obstructionistic behavior by either team must be computed entirely, even in fractions of seconds. Makeup time shall always be ordered in its entirety even in the case when, in the opinion of the referee, a team has been able to preserve a favorable score by persisting in an obstructionistic conduct and lack of discipline.

4. Q. Can the position of the ball affect the end of each half?

   A. The position of the ball is never the determining factor in whistling the end of each half. The end is called even when the ball is not in play.

5. Q. Can the interval of five minutes between the two periods be extended?

A. The interval (five minutes) can be extended in the opinion of the referee to a maximum of fifteen minutes.

6. Q. In case the first or second half is extended (after the expiration of a normal period) to permit a penalty-kick to be taken, or retaken, when shall the penalty-kick procedure terminate?

A. When the duration of the normal play (period) is extended (at the end of the first or second half) to permit the taking or retaking of a penalty-kick, the time extension must last until the moment the penalty-kick has been completed, that is when:

a. the ball goes direct into goal. A goal is scored and the match ends the moment the ball passes wholly the goal-line (see Diagram 34, Page 185);

b. the ball rebounds from either goal-post or cross-bar into goal. A goal is scored and the match ends the moment the ball passes wholly over the goal-line;

c. the ball passes out of play outside the goal-posts or over the cross-bar. The match ends the moment the ball passes beyond the boundary of the field of play;

d. the ball strikes a goal-post or the cross-bar and rebounds into play. The match is terminated the moment the ball rebounds into play;

e. the ball having been touched by the goalkeeper enters the goal. A goal is scored and the match ends the moment the ball passes wholly over the goal line;

f. the ball is clearly saved by the goalkeeper. The referee should whistle for "time" at once. Should the goalkeeper, by mischance, then drop the ball over his goal-line, it is not a goal, for the game has ended;

g. the ball is stopped during its trajectory by an outside agent. The game shall be further extended to allow the penalty-kick to be taken properly;

h. finally, if a defending player infringes the law and encroaches (inside the penalty-area), the play shall be further extended for the penalty-kick to be retaken under the provisions of this law.

7. Q. A player ejected from the game refuses to leave the field of play immediately, despite the prodding of his captain or his club's official and at last, some time later, he goes out of the field. What shall the referee do with regard to the computation of time lost?

A. The referee must make up the lost time entirely (even every second), for it was a case of individual (a player) not collective (a team) disciplinary act.

8. Q. If a player intentionally engages in kicking the ball persistently beyond the side-lines so that he deliberately delays the game or causes loss of time, what actions shall the referee take?

A. The referee should regard such behavior as misconduct and caution the guilty player, as well as record all time lost. In case of the player's persistence in such misconduct, the referee shall eject him from the game. If the play is stopped for such reason, it shall be resumed with an indirect free-kick in favor of the opposing team from the spot where the infringement of the law occurred.

Cases on Law 8
"The Start of Play"

Chapter 11

1. **Q.** Is the choice of ends or of the kick-off compulsory? How and who makes the choice?

   A. The choice is compulsory and must be made by the referee in the presence of the two captains by the toss of a coin or other suitable means. The coin shall be dropped to the ground and retrieved by the referee.

2. **Q.** Who has the priority of choosing "head" or "tail"?

   A. The captain of the guest team (in Europe it is usually the second listed team).

3. **Q.** Before the start of the game, can the captain change his mind over the choice of ends or of the kick-off after manifesting it?

   A. No. Once the choice is made it is final.

4. **Q.** In case extra periods are played, which team shall take the kick-off?

   A. The choice of ends or of the kick-off shall be made "ex-novo." (See 1.)

5. **Q.** What obligations do teams have prior to the start of the game?

   A. The captain of each team, when entering the field, must courteously salute the referee and the captain of the opposing team. Also the team should salute the spectators; this practice should be enforced by the competent league or association.

6. **Q.** If a foreign body (or object) crops up on the field of play a short time before the scheduled kick-off of an official game, what shall the referee do?

A. The referee shall request the captain of the home team to clear the field of play as soon as possible. Whenever the referee is sure the inconvenience has not been artfully contrived and that the home team promptly proceeds to clear the field, he must wait until the job (of clearing the field) is completed and is aware that, even because of a delayed kick-off, the game can be normally played to completion. No rule makes provision as to the time the referee must wait, but it is up to his discretion; he must, however, make sure the players are on the field ready to play, and the identification procedure has taken place prior to the official kick-off time. The players, therefore, shall remain on the field at the referee's disposal.

7. Q. What action shall the referee take if a team refuses to start the game?

A. Should a team refuse to start a game, the referee shall request a written statement from the captain. If the captain refuses to honor such request, the referee shall only take into account the captain's oral statement which will stand, final and irreversible, for the captain cannot subsequently change his prior decision. Therefore the referee shall leave the field at once after notifying the captain of the opposing team.

8. Q. Are the players required to take certain predetermined positions on the field in order to start the game?

A. No. The two teams can deploy their players in any position or role as long as they remain in their own half of the playing field. Furthermore the players of the team not taking the kick-off must remain in their own half and at least a distance of 9.15 m. (10 yards) from the ball.

9. Q. When is the kick-off invalid? What actions should be taken?

A. The kick-off is not valid when the following occur;
a. the ball has not been played as by the rule, i.e., the ball has been played backward or laterally or for a distance less than its circumference;
b. the players move into the opponents' half before the ball has been played according to the rules;
c. the opponents move toward the ball, or encroach at a distance of less than the required 9.15 m. (10 yards) before it has been regularly played;
d. the ball is twice played by the same player before covering a distance equal to its circumference.

When the above cases occur, the kick-off shall be repeated; if the player commits the same violation he shall be cautioned. If a third violation is committed, the player shall be ejected and replaced only when the kick-off is taken to start the first half, but not the second half.

10. Q. When is the precise time the players can run into their opponents' half?

A. The players can run into their opponents' half after the ball has been properly played (see the rule). When an infraction occurs, the kick-off shall be repeated. If a player persists in infringing the rule he must be cautioned and subsequently ejected if he has repeated the infraction. The same procedure must be followed when resuming the play after a goal has been scored.

11. Q. Can an individual (outsider) other than a player kick the ball to start the game?

A. No. However, only in case of a friendly game an outsider can kick the ball to start the game. Afterwards the ball will immediately be brought back to the center of the field and the kick-off can then be taken according to the rules.

12. Q. A team wins the toss of the coin and chooses the kick-off. At the precise end of the first half the same team suffers a goal, but because the time has expired play cannot resume. Which team is entitled to take the kick-off for the second half?

A. The kick-off to start the second half must be taken by the team that did not start the game (first half).

13. Q. If the player kicks off the ball and immediately touches it with his hands before it is ever touched by another player, what action should the referee take?

A. The play shall immediately be stopped and then resumed with a direct free-kick from the precise spot where the infraction occurred by a player of the opposing team, provided the ball was originally played according to the rules. In any other case, the kick-off must be retaken.

14. Q. A teammate of the player taking the kick-off touches the ball before it has traveled a distance equal to its circumference. What action shall the referee take?

A. The referee shall stop the play and repeat the kick-off.

15. Q. Following a kick-off the ball goes directly into the opponents' net (goal). What decision should the referee take?

A. The goal is not valid. The play shall be resumed by the opposing team with a goal-kick.

16. Q. What distance should the players observe when the referee drops the ball?

A. Any distance as long as they do not interfere with the normal procedure followed by the referee and any two opponents in contention for the ball.

17. Q. Where will the referee drop the ball when, at the time the play was stopped, the ball was anywhere inside the playing field?

A. If the referee must stop the play while the ball is anywhere within the playing field, touch-lines (including the segment between the goal-posts), he shall drop the ball on the precise spot of the perimetral lines. Since there are no required distances to be observed by the players, it is perfectly satisfactory that the ball touch the ground, even on the touch-line, in order to be played by any player.

18. Q. Following the referee's dropping of the ball, as soon as it touches the ground the ball is kicked by a player directly into the goal. Is the goal valid?

A. Yes. No matter which player has kicked the ball (either a defending or an attacking player), as long as the ball has traveled a distance of 70 cm. after touching the ground and before crossing the goal-line.

19. Q. While the referee is dropping the ball and before it is in play an infraction is committed. What shall the referee do?

A. The referee will drop the ball once again but only after taking any disciplinary actions

20. Q. What shall the referee do if a player persistently plays the ball before it is in play (has touched the ground)?

A. At the second violation the referee shall caution the player, and subsequently eject him from the game if he persists in the same wrongdoing. In any case, the play shall be resumed by the referee who shall again drop the ball instead of awarding an indirect free-kick for the ejection of the player, because the infraction occurred when the play had not normally resumed.

21. Q. Following a temporary stoppage of play due to various reasons, how shall play be resumed?

A. If the play had stopped after the ball crossed the touch-line or after enforcing any rule or regulation, it shall be resumed according to the rules of the game. If play has stopped due to various causes, it shall be resumed by the referee who shall drop the ball on the same spot where it was at the time of the stoppage of play.

Cases on Law 9
"Ball In and Out of Play"

Chapter 12

1. Q. What does the expression "ball in play" actually mean?

   A. The expression "ball in play" simply means that the ball can produce valid technical actions of a play.

2. Q. If the ball has crossed the goal-line or the touch-line only in part, should it be deemed "not in play"?

   A. No. The ball must entirely clear the goal-line or the touch-line in order to be considered "not in play." (See Diagram 34, p. 185.)

3. Q. Should the referee whistle any stoppage and resumption of play?

   A. The referee must whistle and stop the play every time he has to administer either a technical or a disciplinary sanction, when an injured player needs assistance, to eject unauthorized individuals or remove objects from the field, to validate a goal just scored, to order a kick-off or the resumption of play after a goal has been scored, to signal a penalty-kick, to call the end of the first or second half of the match, to order a minute of attention (of someone's death, etc.). It is not necessary that the referee whistle every time the ball crosses the touch-lines or when a free-kick is taken (as long as the resumption of play is immediate and there are no objections as to the distance—9.15 m., or 10 yards—to be observed), a corner-kick, a throw-in, a drop of the ball (by the referee).

4. Q. A player asks the referee to be allowed to leave the field. On his way out and before crossing the field's markings he plays the ball and scores a goal. What is the referee's decision?

A. The player will be cautioned; the play will be stopped and then resumed by granting an indirect free-kick to the opposing team on the exact spot where the infraction occurred. The goal, of course is disallowed.

5. Q. While the ball is outside the field's boundary lines or during a temporary suspension of the play, should technical cautions be given by the referee?

A. The answer is no. When the ball is not in play, only disciplinary sanctions can be imposed (cautions or ejections from the field).

6. Q. The ball goes outside the field of play or into a goal after striking either the referee or an official linesman. What is the referee's decision?

A. Since the physical presence on the field of play of either the referee or the official linesmen can only be of authorized people, as far as the play is concerned their presence cannot therefore be regarded as that of foreign elements; when the ball accidentally strikes any of them, not so much a linesman who must perform outside the boundary lines, but usually the referee, the play is not altered in any way.

7. Q. After striking the referee the ball crosses the touch-line (leaves the field). The referee is unable to determine which player played the ball last. Which side should take the throw-in?

A. The referee shall seek the opinion of the linesman, if an official one, closest to the play and will rely on his judgment. Whenever even the linesman is unable to indicate which side should take the throw-in, the referee shall decide in favor of the defending team.

8. Q. The referee blows the whistle by mistake or accidentally. What should he do?

A. Since by blowing the whistle the referee has stopped the play, he shall resume it by dropping the ball on the exact spot where the ball was at the time the play was interrupted.

9. Q. While the ball is in play, a whistle similar to that of the referee is heard from a stranger. The players stop playing, waiting for the referee's decision. What should the referee decide?

A. The referee shall disregard the whistle coming from a stranger. However he shall quickly direct the players, by appropriate gestures or by voice to continue playing (usually urging . . . "play on.")

10. Q. During the progress of a play, the ball is intentionally played or stopped by an unofficial linesman. What should the referee's decision be?

A. The referee shall immediately stop the play and eject the guilty linesman who must be replaced, then he will resume the play by dropping the ball on the exact spot where it was at the time it was illegally played. The incident shall be reported to the competent league or association.

11. Q. The ball hits the pole of a corner flag breaking it and knocking it down, but it remains inside the field of play. Should the referee stop the play or allow it to proceed?

A. The referee shall stop the play and have the corner flag replaced. He shall then drop the ball on the exact spot where it was at the time the play was stopped.

12. Q. Following a resumption of play, the referee realizes, personally or upon indication by an official linesman, that the same, i.e., the resumption of play has not been the one required by the official rules and regulations for the case which has determined the stoppage of play. What should the referee's decision be?

A. The resumption of play already made cannot be altered, unless the referee intervenes with obvious quickness and expeditiousness. The referee, in any case, should report the incident.

13. Q. For reasons beyond his control, the referee is unable to blow the whistle as quickly as required to stop the play. How shall the referee decide?

A. If it appeared to be impossible to blow the whistle, the referee shall call the players' attention, by voice or by motions, and indicate to them that he intended to stop the play, then he shall resume it as the case will require. However, if the referee has been unable to blow the whistle due to sudden indisposition, all subsequent play shall be disregarded. Whenever the referee is able to resume officiating, the play shall be resumed as by the kind of stoppage discerned just prior to the indisposition.

Cases on Law 10
"Method of Scoring"

Chapter 13

1. Q. When should a goal be regarded as duly scored?

 A. When an officially approved ball shall entirely cross the goal-line between the goal-posts and below the cross-bar on the ground or in the air, provided no violation of rules has occurred by the attacking team prior to the scoring. A goal can be scored by a goalkeeper standing inside his penalty area by propelling the ball with his hands. If a defending player touches the ball with his hands but does not stop it, the goal is valid.

2. Q. When, according to the rules of the game, is a goal not valid?

 A. When the goal has been scored:
   a. directly on a kick-off, on a goal-kick, on a throw-in; the play shall be resumed with a goal-kick or with a corner-kick if a defending player has scored against his own goal;
   b. kicking directly toward own goal from a free-kick, direct or indirect; the play shall be resumed by ordering a corner-kick or repeating the free-kick if the same was made from inside the penalty-area and the ball had not crossed over the area before it went into goal;
   c. directly from the referee's dropping of the ball (he shall repeat it);
   d. when due to a foreign body or object; in this case the play shall be resumed by the referee who will drop the ball on the exact spot where the ball was played last except when a penalty shot is involved (which must be retaken);
   e. immediately after the ball has been found to be irregular, deflated or otherwise; the play shall be resumed by the referee

with a new official ball which he will drop on the exact spot where the irregularity of the previous ball was first detected.

3. Q. The referee has allowed a goal. The captain of the team suffering the goal complains about some irregularity in the scoring of the goal and requests the referee to consult the officially appointed linesman. What shall the referee do?

A. The referee is free to request an opinion of the official linesman, whenever he deems necessary, and in all those cases he has been unable to follow a play very closely, or he has not detected any playing irregularity which requires a disciplinary sanction; in any case, never under any player's protest or urging. However, whenever in doubt and only on his own initiative, the referee shall request the opinion of the officially appointed linesman who has been closer to the play and accept his judgment as final.

4. Q. The goalkeeper, while trying to gain control of the ball, grasps the cross-bar displacing it or knocking it down while the ball goes into goal nonetheless. Is the goal valid? In case the ball does not go into goal due to the presence of the cross-bar on the ground, which interferes with the scoring, what shall the referee do?

A. In the former case, the goal is valid and the goalkeeper shall be officially cautioned (ungentlemanly conduct); in the second case, the referee shall immediately stop the play, caution the goalkeeper and order an indirect free-kick to the opposing team.

5. Q. The ball appears to be irregular immediately after crossing the goal-line (between the goal-posts and beneath the cross-bar). What decision shall the referee take?

A. Whenever the referee is positively certain that the ball's irregularity occurred an instant before the same crossed the goal-line, he shall disallow the goal and resume the play by dropping the ball where the former ball was at the time it became irregular (deflated or the like). If the ball's irregularity was detected after it crossed the goal-line, the goal shall be valid.

6. Q. If the referee validates a goal before the ball has completely cleared the goal-line and realizes he has erred, is the goal valid?

A. The goal is not valid. The play shall be resumed by the referee who will drop the ball on the exact spot it was when the play was first erroneously stopped.

7. Q. The goalkeeper appears to be clearly beaten. However, just before the ball crosses the goal-line a spectator enters the field of play and tries, unsuccessfully, to stop it on the goal-line. What action shall the referee take?

A. If the ball has not been touched, the goal must be allowed, otherwise, the referee, after clearing the field of play of the intruder shall drop the ball on the spot where it was at the time it was touched.

Cases on Law 11
"Off-Side"

Chapter 14

1. Q. When is the exact moment and when shall an off-side be called?

    A. The position of off-side shall be determined at the moment when a playmate, in an irregular position plays the ball. A ball is considered played when, following either a heading or a kicking, it travels any distance, even minimal. Once the referee has ascertained the position of an off-side he shall intervene, but only when the player (in an off-side position) is actively participating in the play, interferes with an opponent, or tries to take advantage of his irregular position.

2. Q. A forward has two or more opponents between himself and the opponents' goal-line, while a player of his own side passes the ball to him; but when the ball gets to him there is only one opponent (the goalkeeper or nobody else). Is the position of the forward to be considered an off-side (when he gets control of the ball)?

    A. No, for at the time the ball was passed to him by a player of his own side his position was not off-side.

3. Q. Is a player off-side if he is on the same imaginary line of the ball when it is being played by a teammate?

    A. No. By being on the same line as the ball, he cannot be closer than the ball to the opponents' goal-line.

4. Q. Must a player in an off-side position be penalized if he does not actively participate in the play?

A. No. The off-side position of a player not actively involved in a play is not punishable, unless the referee determines that the player's seemingly passive position interferes in some way.

5. Q. Is there an off-side when the ball remains on the field of play after hitting the goal-posts or the referee?

A. Yes. If the ball bounces off the goal-posts or touches the referee and then goes to a playmate of the forward who first kicked it, it is as if it was directly passed by one player to another. Thus, if the player who gets the ball was in an off-side position, even though he has not directly participated in the play, he shall be penalized by the referee who will stop the play and grant an indirect free-kick to the defending team.

6. Q. Should a player be considered in an off-side position if he is standing on the halfway line having only one opponent between himself and the opponent goal-line?

A. No. Since the halfway line belongs to both sides of the field of play, the player standing right on it must be considered as if he is standing on his own half field.

7. Q. Can a player who is off-side put himself on side by coming back on his own half-field in order to gain possession of the ball?

A. No. (See Diagram 23, p. 174.)

8. Q. Can a player who is off-side put himself on side? (See Diagram 14, p. 165.)

A. As long as a teammate continues to play and maintain control of the ball, the player in an off-side position can put himself on side, provided the referee does not detect any interference with the play of the opponents by the player in the off-side position. The same player can also automatically be put on side by the teammate who is in possession of the ball and finds himself behind the playmate on an ideal (imaginary) line parallel to the opposing goal-line.

9. Q. A forward who is initially in a not punishable off-side position, suddenly finds himself on side not on his initiative. A player of his side who is in possession of the ball, having noticed the on-side position of the forward (teammate) passes the ball to him. Should the referee penalize the player and call the off-side?

A. No. The changed position of the defending players—as well as of his teammate in possession of the ball—has corrected the initially irregular position of the forward.

10. Q. While playing the ball, a forward falls down leaving the ball in a less forward position, i.e., a little back; subsequently he gets up and replays the ball. Is there an off-side?

A. No. The play is perfectly normal.

11. Q. Can a player in an off-side position cross a side-line or a goal-line to avoid being penalized?

A. Yes, he can. However he must re-enter the field of play away from the action. If he delays coming back into the field of play, standing outside it, he must re-enter as soon as the play stops.

12. Q. Does a player violate the off-side rule when being in an off-side position he crosses any part of the perimetral lines of the playground to show to the referee that he wants to stay off the play and not interfere with it?

A. No. However if the referee feels that the player's moves have a tactical purpose or appear to be fake in any way, and the player immediately thereafter takes part in the play, he must be penalized; for although not participating in the play he was indirectly but actively involved.

13. Q. Realizing he is off-side a forward places himself inside the opponents' goal and outside the field of play where he waits, albeit passively, the end of the play. Meantime a teammate scores a goal. Should this goal be allowed or disallowed, assuming the player standing inside the goal has interfered with the goalkeeper?

A. If the forward player has not actually interfered—by words or motions— with the goalkeeper, the goal is valid. Otherwise the referee must stop the play immediately, caution the player standing inside the goal for ungentlemanly conduct and then resume the play by dropping the ball on the exact spot where it was at the time the play was interrupted.

14. Q. Should an off-side be called if it has been deliberately created by a defenseman who has left the field of play or has placed himself inside the goal?

A. No. In such a case the defenseman must be cautioned for ungentlemanly conduct as soon as the play stops.

15. Q. A forward is found standing on a line parallel to the goal- line with one or more opponents while a teammate is playing the ball and having only the goalkeeper in front of him. Is he off-side?

A. Yes, because he does not have at least two opponents between himself and the opposing goal-line.*

16. Q. A free-kick is taken. A forward joins the opponents who are in the process of setting up a barrier in front of the goalie, among them or beside one of them on a line parallel to the goal-line or right on it, beyond which there is only the goalkeeper. Is the player off-side?

---

*This rule no longer applies, for the off-side does not exist.

A. Yes, because he is actively participating in the play and does not have at least two players between himself and the opposing goal-line.

17. Q. In the case of either a free-kick or a penalty-kick, can there be off-side?

A. Yes. In either of these cases there can be off-side and the rule is fully enforced.

18. Q. When taking a corner-kick, a goal-kick, a throw-in, dropping the ball by the referee and when the ball is last played by an opponent, when do the exceptions to the rule on off-side cease to exist?

A. As soon as a teammate of the player in an off-side position touches the ball.

19. Q. After taking a corner-kick or a throw-in, can a player move in a position behind the play in order to avoid the off-side?

A. Yes, so long as the player in question is not in an off-side position at the time a teammate plays the ball.

20. Q. Can a player in an off-side position be put on side at the precise moment the ball is last played by an opponent?

A. The off-side position of a player is corrected by the intervention of a defenseman who gets possession of the ball, provided the referee is convinced that the forward was not actively involved in the play. Otherwise the off-side must be called even though the referee's whistling may not be timely.

21. Q. A forward in an off-side position, undetected by the referee, is about to get possession of the ball passed to him by a playmate. A defenseman, anticipating the referee's whistle (calling for the off-side), deliberately grabs the ball with his hands stopping the play. What decision should the referee take?

A. The referee shall stop the play and assess a direct free-kick (for the handball) or penalty kick if the infraction occurred anywhere inside the penalty-area.

22. Q. A forward passes the ball to a teammate who is off-side and is detected by the referee. Before the play is stopped, however, a player on the defending team intentionally plays the ball with his hands but does not prevent it from getting to the opponent (forward) who is off-side. Which decision must the referee take?

A. The referee shall penalize only the off-side, even though his whistle was not timely.

Cases on Law 12
"Fouls and Misconduct"

Chapter 15

1. Q. In what way should intentionality be considered, for it is the fundamental condition in judging all the fouls contemplated in the first part of Law 12?

    A. Intentionality in committing a foul must be the intended actual and deliberate will to commit the foul, independently from the reason which motivated it and from the attainment, or not, of the end the (guilty) player had originally intended. Thus it does not constitute an excuse for a player to deliberately play the ball with the hand assuming the referee is going to call some previously committed infraction, or that the player has deliberately, though unsuccessfully, charged an opponent with the apparent intent to hurt him. In short: it is enough, and sufficiently so, that a player with clear and manifest willingness play or touch the ball with the hand—or with the arm—or intervene against an opponent in a way not permitted by the rules and regulations to regard the foul as intentionally committed. In the case of a handball, the foul is not penalized if it has been committed clearly with the purpose of instinctively protecting the face or the lower abdomen from a hard- kicked ball.

2. Q. In which cases is intentionality found when a player uses the hands, or arms, in order to play the ball?

    A. When a player uses his hands to touch the ball and when he lifts high or spreads the arms in order to interrupt the trajectory of the ball more effectively. Whenever, in a free-kick situation, the players of the defending team form a barrier but cover more space by stretching the arms wide; any foul which may derive following the free-kick must be regarded as deliberate. It is well to remember that intentional and repeated use of the hands by the same player constitutes misconduct and can result in an official caution.

3. Q. In what way does a foul start?

A. The actual start of a foul must be found only in a case of a violent conduct committed at a distance, such as spitting, throwing a stone, throwing a soccer shoe or any object. In any of the above cases, the infraction has occurred on the spot where the guilty player committed the foul.

In cases of contact fouls, i.e., when a player strikes an opponent, the exact spot where the foul starts is one and the same as that where the contact was first made. In the case of a handball, the point of contact of the hand or the arm and the ball is where the infraction occurred.

4. Q. The ball kicked by a forward would surely end in a goal with the goalie completely cut off from the play if it didn't bounce back from a defenseman's arm inside the penalty area. Although the contact of the ball with the player's arm was not intentional, even though it has averted a sure goal, should the referee assess a penalty kick?

A. Since the contact with the ball was not made intentionally, irrespective of the ensuing consequences, the foul (handball) is in effect actually not existent; therefore it cannot be punished.

5. Q. A player stops the ball with the hand thinking that an opponent has committed a foul or the referee has stopped the play. What decision should the referee reach?

A. The referee shall assess a direct free-kick or a penalty-kick.

6. Q. A player leans against an opponent in order to get possession of the ball. What is the referee's decision?

A. Such act constitutes a foul (holding or pushing an opponent); it must, therefore, be punished by a direct free-kick or penalty-kick.

7. Q. A player, away from a play occurring near his goal-area, strikes an opponent standing beside him. What is the referee's decision?

A. Except where the advantage rule applies, the referee must immediately eject the guilty player and assess a direct free-kick or a penalty-kick to the opposing team from the spot where the foul occurred.

8 .Q. Should the referee assess a penalty-kick when a player of the defending team is ejected because of having stricken an opponent inside his penalty-area?

A. Yes, so long as the infraction has occurred while the ball was in play.

9. Q. Two players of the same team intentionally sandwich an opponent impeding him from continuing playing the ball or getting possession of it. What shall the referee do?

A. Since the infraction is the same as holding an opponent, the referee shall assess a direct free-kick or a penalty-kick.

10. Q. If a player, inside his own penalty-area and while the ball is in play, trips or strikes an opponent who is in an off-side position undetected by the referee, should a penalty-kick be assessed?

A. Yes.

11. Q. A defenseman, inside his own penalty-area, intentionally plays the ball with the hands sending it, nonetheless, into goal. Should the goal be valid?

A. Yes, As a matter of fact, if the referee should punish the infraction with a penalty-kick he would give an advantage to the team guilty of the infraction. However if the referee stops the play before the ball crosses the goal-line, he must assess the penalty-kick.

12. Q. If the goalkeeper intentionally plays the ball with his hands outside his own penalty-area or runs outside it with the ball in his hands, what decision should the referee take?

A. The referee shall assess a direct free-kick in favor of the opposing team.

13. Q. After the referee has whistled a resumption (any) of the play, but before the ball is played properly, a player touches the ball with the hand. Should the infraction be punished?

A. No. Since the ball was touched by the player's hand before the play had resumed, the referee shall not penalize the infraction but shall urge the resumption of the play solicitously according to the manner required by the case which first determined the stoppage.

14. Q. A player of the defending team intentionally touches the ball with his hands while it is standing or rolling on the line marking the penalty-area. How should the referee penalize the infraction?

A. Since the ball is still on the line marking the penalty-area and, therefore, inside the area, the referee shall assess a penalty-kick.

15. Q. If a defending player other than the goalkeeper, while standing outside his own penalty-area, intentionally uses his hands to play the ball which is inside the area, what shall the referee decide?

A. Since the violation has occurred inside the penalty-area, he shall assess a penalty-kick.

16. Q. A player attempts to play the ball intentionally with his hands unsuccessfully. Should he be penalized?

A. No. He cannot be penalized for attempting to play the ball with his hands, for no penalty is contemplated in the rules and regulations regarding such attempt.

17. Q. A player, allowed by the referee to leave the playground due to a slight incident or other cause, remains standing right on the touch-line and, by stretching a leg inside the field causes an opponent to fall down. What decision should the referee take?

A. Since the infraction has occurred inside the playing field, the guilty player must be cautioned and the play resumed with a direct free-kick or a penalty-kick.

18. Q. A player, re-entering into the field or coming late to the game, joins the play without the referee's permission or consent and commits a more serious infraction (plays the ball with the hand or strikes an opponent). Which infraction should the referee punish the player for?

A. He must be penalized for the more serious infraction, as well as cautioned for entering the field of play without the referee's consent.

19. Q. Two opposing players are standing outside the touch-line inside the specially-marked two-yard area. One of the two players commits a foul against the other while the ball is in play. What shall the referee do?

A. Provided the advantage rule is applicable, the referee must immediately stop the play, caution or eject (as the case may require) the guilty player, and then resume the play by dropping the ball on the exact spot where it was when the play was called.

20. Q. Two players of the same team commit two infractions simultaneously. What shall the referee decide?

A. He shall punish the more serious infraction and shall also take disciplinary actions, where required.

21. Q. Two opposing players commit two infractions simultaneously. What is the referee's decision?

A. In the case of two infractions of different nature (and seriousness), the referee shall punish the more serious offense. If the two infractions are of the same nature, the referee shall assess a free-kick (direct or indirect, as the case may require) to the defending team, and take disciplinary actions if necessary. Whenever the infractions occur about the half-way line, the referee shall assess a free-kick to the team that, to his sole judgment, appeared to be the defending one.

22. Q. During the half-time intermission, a player strikes an opponent or is guilty of violent conduct toward anyone in the presence of the referee or of an official linesman. What action shall the referee take?

A. He shall inhibit the guilty player from further participation in the contest; he shall not, obviously, be replaced for the remainder of the game.

23. Q. A player strikes an opponent while the referee is about to drop the ball but before the same touches the ground. How shall the referee resume the play?

A. After assessing the required disciplinary punishment for the infraction (striking an opponent), the referee shall resume the play by dropping the ball. Since the ball was not in play at the time the infraction occurred, the referee cannot award a free-kick.

24. Q. Which acts cause dangerous play and how must they be penalized?

A. Dangerous play is determined by those acts, although committed with no intention of causing physical injury, can nonetheless in the opinion of the referee be dangerous both to the player who commits them as well as to his teammates or opponents. For instance to kick or attempting to kick the ball with the leg raised as high as anyone's face, with both feet simultaneously, with a slide, from behind, with a double-kick, while the ball is held by the goalie and while he is kicking it. Furthermore to jump raising the knee forward while an opponent is very close.

A dangerous play, even self-inflicted, is penalized with an indirect free-kick. The infraction cannot be charged against the goalkeeper who reaches for the ball by sliding toward the player's feet in order to get possession of the ball.

25. Q. Is a player allowed to tackle an opponent who is playing the ball by sliding toward it with both feet simultaneously?

A. No. Being dangerous play it must be penalized with an indirect free-kick. However, if in such a play the referee discerns an intimidating behavior or, in any case, an excessive athletic exuberance, he must caution the guilty player.

In the case of a player hitting an opponent intentionally with both feet while he is playing the ball the referee shall eject him (guilty player) from the field and assess a direct free-kick, or penalty-kick, to the opposing team.

26. Q. A goalie, while in the process of grabbing the ball, raises a knee or stretches a leg forward while the opponent is close by. Should he be penalized?

A. Yes. He must be penalized for dangerous play. If the referee notices a deliberate attempt in the goalie's play to strike an opponent, he shall eject the goalie from the game and award a penalty-kick.

27. Q. How must fair or unfair charge be interpreted (understood)?

A. A fair charge is intended to be a push made shoulder against shoulder against an opponent within playing range of the ball or while playing it, as long as it is not violent or dangerous. All charges made with the chest or against the chest, with a side, with a hip or with an elbow are unfair.

28. Q. What is meant by the expression "playing distance"?

A. "Playing distance" is determined in relation to the dynamics of the play, by the possibility offered a player to immediately play or gain control of the ball.

29. Q. Can a player disregard the ball he is playing in order to charge an opponent?

A. If the opponent is not about to play the ball, the charge shall not be allowed. Consequently the player guilty of charging infraction shall be punished with an indirect free-kick. However, if the charge was violent, the infraction shall be punished with a direct free-kick or a penalty-kick.

30. Q. The ball is inside the penalty-area. A forward, quite a distance from the action, suddenly runs toward the ball trying to get possession of it but a defending player charges him fairly. Is there an infraction?

A. Yes. Since the ball was not within playing distance, the forward player could not have been charged. Thus the referee shall punish the defending player guilty of the infraction with an indirect free-kick. However if the charge was violent, the infraction shall be punished with a direct free-kick from the spot where the foul occurred, or with a penalty-kick if the foul occurred inside the penalty-area.

31. Q. What is meant by the expression "obstruction," and how shall it be punished?

A. "Obstruction" is an intentional, deliberate act of creating an obstacle with a player's own body interposed between the ball—when it is not within playing distance—and an opponent who is moving toward the ball in order to gain control of it. The obstruction is punished with an indirect free-kick. However it the two opposing players collide frontally, there cannot be obstruction but an attempt to hold or to strike an opponent; in such case, the infraction shall be punished with a direct free-kick or a penalty-kick.

32. Q. The ball is rolling toward a touch-line or a goal-line while a defending player follows it, remaining within playing distance of the ball about to leave the field of play. An opposing forward (player) attempting to gain possession of the ball charges the opponent with the shoulder. Is there an infraction?

A. No, for the opponent was actually obstructing and in such cases he can be charged fairly, but never violently.

33. Q. In what manner should a charge with the shoulder be made?

A. By charging the opponent on the area of the shoulder but not in the back. The charge toward the area of the spine is obviously extremely dangerous and it is forbidden in any circumstances. Thus it shall be punished with an indirect free-kick, or a penalty-kick, and the guilty player ejected from the game at once.

34. Q. When can a goalie be charged?

A. When he is in possession of the ball or obstructs an opponent or when he is outside his own goal-area.

35. Q. What shall the referee do in the case of a forward who comes in contact with the opposing goalie, who is not in possession of the ball inside the goal-area?

A. If the referee detects the deliberate intention to obstruct the goalie in the play of the forward player, he must assess an indirect free-kick (to the defending team).

36. Q. A goalie, inside his own goal area, drops the ball he was holding in his hands in order to kick it. Can he be charged?

A. No. Since the goalie does not have the ball in his possession (hands) and is inside his own goal-area, he cannot be charged. Whenever a forward player charges the goalie, he shall be punished with an indirect free-kick.

37. Q. How can a goalie commit an infraction while playing the ball? How shall the infraction be punished?

A. The goalie can get possession of the ball with his hands, carrying it, or bouncing it on the ground or in the air, taking one or more steps; he can subsequently replay the ball with his feet and, at last, retaking it with his hands and getting rid of it for good, as long as the number of steps taken while holding the ball with the hands is not more than four.* Thus the goalie commits an infraction if he is playing the ball inside his own goal-area:

*A goalie is now allowed to take more than four steps as long as he doesn't delay the game.

a. holds the ball in his hands while taking more than four steps;*
b. bounces the ball on the field or up in the air and retakes it after taking more than four steps and does not get rid of it so that it can be played by another player;
c. makes moves which, in the opinion of the referee, have the evident purpose of delaying the game.

The infraction by the goalie must be punished with an indirect free-kick from the exact spot where the infraction was committed.

38. Q. What is meant by "recidivity"?

A. The repeated infractions of the rules of the game, indefinite and not necessarily specific, committed by the same player.

39. Q. Which acts constitute "misconduct" and how should they be dealt with?

A. "Misconduct" should be regarded as all those acts and behaviors contrary to the spirit of the game. For example, when repeatedly violating the rules of the game, making remarks, protests, or behaving disrespectfully toward the referee or official linesmen; attempting to fool an opponent by yelling "ball"; disturbing or distracting the opponents' play by means of screams or gestures at the resumption of play; simulating a foul; resorting to expedients with the obvious purpose of delaying the game; kicking away the ball deliberately, or refusing to respect the 9.15 m. (10 yards) distance rule in order to delay the taking of a free-kick or a corner-kick; holding the ball with the legs or lying on it; leaving the field of play—except in the case of an injury—or re-entering the playground without the expressed assent of the referee; leaning on a teammate in order to jump higher; grabbing the cross-bar attempting to lower it; and so on. All acts of misconduct require a caution in any case. If a player already cautioned for any infractions is guilty of misconduct he must be sent off the field. If the play has been stopped by the referee in order to caution or eject a player, the play shall be resumed with an indirect free-kick against the guilty player's team from the spot where the infraction occurred.

40. Q. How should a caution be administered?

A. Normally the referee must administer it to the involved player when the play is dead, noting on his game-card the player's number (name), the exact time of the infraction, and the reasons behind the decision. However in order to avoid possible outbreaks of violence or incidents,

---

*See footnote on p. 64.

fully considering the environmental (crowd) conditions, the referee can depart from the usual procedure by administering the caution to the player involved while the play is in progress (informing him of his decision) by approaching him briefly. In such a case, the referee shall take all due notices on his game-card as soon as he finds it feasible.

41. Q. A player, even if tardy, while standing right outside the touch-line or a goal-line and play is still in progress, (he) stretches any part of his body and touches the ball inside the field. What is the referee's decision?

A. The player shall be considered as having entered, or re-entered, the playground without the required permission of the referee. Thus unless the advantage rule is applicable, he shall be cautioned and punished with an indirect free-kick from the spot where the infraction occurred.

42. Q. A player, while outside the touch-line or a goal-line and waiting to enter or re-enter the field of play, positions himself near the opponent's goal. When the ball suddenly rolls toward him, he stretches a foot and scores a goal. What decision should the referee take?

A. First of all the goal shall be disallowed. Furthermore he shall caution the player who has taken part in the action or rejoined the play without the referee's permission, and shall award an indirect free-kick to the opposing team from the spot on the touch-line or goal-line that the player crossed.

43. Q. In the same instance, as outlined in question 42, a player takes position near his goal and in order to avoid the scoring of a goal by the other side enters the field of play and stops the ball with the hand inside his own penalty-area. What decision shall the referee take?

A. The referee shall caution the player and assess a penalty-kick.

44. Q. A player coming late to the game or re-entering the field of play takes part in the play without the express consent of the referee and scores a goal. What decision should the referee take?

A. If the referee feels absolutely certain, before the play resumes, that the player has entered the field of play immediately prior to taking the shot, he shall disallow the goal and resume the play by awarding an indirect free-kick to the opposing team from the exact spot where the infringement, by the above mentioned player, occurred. If the referee instead cannot be absolutely certain about the exact moment the guilty player entered the field of play, he shall allow the goal. In either case, he shall caution the guilty player and report him to the competent league or association.

45. Q. In the same circumstances as described in the preceding (44), a player kicks the ball into his own goal. What is the referee's decision?

A. He shall validate the goal and caution the player guilty of the infraction.

46. Q. Still in the same circumstances as described above (44 and 45), a player plays or attempts to play the ball but does not succeed in preventing the scoring of a goal by the opposition. What is the referee's decision?

A. The referee shall allow the goal and caution the player guilty of the infraction.

47. Q. Can a player conspicuously show dissent from any decision by the referee by means of words or gestures?

A. No. The referee must caution the guilty player and, unless the advantage rule is applicable, he shall punish the guilty player by assessing an indirect free-kick to the opposing team.

48. Q. A player leaves the field of play as a protest against a referee's decision. How should the referee deal with such a behavior?

A. The player must be regarded as having been ejected. The referee, unable to notify his decision to the guilty player, shall inform the captain as soon as the play stops. The incident must be reported by the referee.

  If the player re-enters the field of play while the play is in progress, the referee shall immediately stop the play, shall notify his decision to him and then restart the play by dropping the ball; the ejected player is regarded as a stranger.

49. Q. A defenseman, while outside his own penalty-area, strikes an opponent standing in the same general area, or hits him with a stone. What decision shall the referee take?

A. Since the throwing of a stone or any other object constitutes "violent conduct," the referee shall eject the guilty player and restart the play with an indirect free-kick from the spot where the infraction occurred.

50. Q. A goalkeeper, unable to do otherwise, tries to stop the trajectory of the ball which is about to cross the goal-line, by using a stone or some other object. What decision shall the referee take?

A. The referee shall stop the play and caution the goalie guilty of ungentlemanly conduct. Then he shall assess an indirect free-kick to the opposing team from the spot where the throwing of the object occurred. Of course, if the ball goes entirely beyond the goal-line, the goal is valid.

51. Q. A player is standing outside the side-lines, or inside the goal, and interferes with an opponent by voice or gestures. Should he be punished?

A. Yes. If the infraction occurs while the ball is in play, the referee shall caution the player guilty of ungentlemanly conduct and, unless the advantage rule is applicable, he shall restart the play by dropping the ball where it was at the time the play was called.

52. Q. Does calling the ball from a teammate constitute an infringement of the laws of the game?

A. No, as long as it does not alter the normal progress of the game; otherwise the referee shall assess an indirect free-kick to the opposing team.

53. Q. After the referee has assessed a free-kick, the guilty player or teammate kicks the ball away as a protest against the referee's decision. What decision shall the referee take?

A. He shall caution the guilty player.

54. Q. The referee has stopped the play to assess an indirect free-kick. Before the free-kick is taken a player of the team being penalized commits a more serious foul punishable with a direct free-kick. Should the referee penalize the more serious offense?

A. No. The indirect free-kick must be taken. Nonetheless if the infraction subsequently committed, but before the play is restarted, calls for the caution or the ejection of the guilty player, the referee shall act accordingly. Thus it is necessary for the referee to always be aware of the reasons which caused the stoppage of the play in the first place, in order to resume it accordingly.

55. Q. What decision shall the referee take if two players of the same team are both guilty of ungentlemanly or violent conduct inside the field of play?

A. The referee shall caution or eject them according to the degree of the infraction committed by either player. If the infraction occurred while the ball was in play, he shall assess an indirect free-kick on behalf of the opposing team.

56. Q. Can the referee omit mentioning in his report the name of a cautioned player who subsequently has apologized?

A. No. The referee must report all cautions administered.

57. Q. What is meant by brutal and by violent conduct? How should they be penalized?

A. By brutal conduct it is meant the commission of any voluntary act with the purpose to cause physical injuries, such as: to strike or attempt to strike an opponent either by kicks, fists, slaps (by hand), heading, etc.

By violent conduct it is meant any act, gesture, behavior, or an expression contrary to the self-possession (self control) and dignity required by all committed to the purity of the sport. Within the

conceptual confines of violent conduct is included the outrageous act of spitting at an opponent, at a game official, at any person authorized to stay close to the playground (press people, etc.) or at any other individual, as well as the insult or the aggression at the referee or at the official linesmen. All acts of brutal and violent conduct require the immediate ejection of the guilty player and the referee shall assess against the guilty player's team:
   a. a direct free-kick, or a penalty-kick in all cases of brutal conduct;
   b. an indirect free-kick in all cases of violent conduct.

58. Q. What decisions should the referee take if a player uses obscene or abusive language, or curses?

A. The referee must eject the guilty player. If the play has been called, it shall be resumed with an indirect free-kick against the guilty player's team from the spot where the infraction occurred.

59. Q. A player insults or strikes the referee or linesman. What decision shall the referee take?

A. Any player who insults, spits at, or strikes a game official is guilty of violent conduct. Therefore he must be ejected. Whenever the play needs to be called in order for the referee to assess the punishment, it must be resumed according to the position of the guilty player:
   a. with an indirect free-kick if the guilty player was inside the field of play;
   b. with the dropping of the ball by the referee if the player was standing outside the field of play.

60. Q. Can a player ejected from the game remain right outside the field of play?

A. No. Before the play is resumed the referee must make sure that the ejected player has left the area surrounding the playground. In case of a refusal, the referee shall request the assistance of the captain of the involved team, but must avoid any argument or discussion.
   If two opposing players are ejected simultaneously, it is advisable that the referee send the players away separately.

61. Q. Can a player be ejected as a precaution against future trouble?

A. No. A player can be ejected only if he has infringed those laws of the game which required such extreme disciplinary action.

62. Q. Can a player be ejected from the game without having previously been cautioned?

A. Yes. In all cases of brutal or violent conduct.

Cases on Law 13
"Free-Kick"

Chapter 16

1. Q. What is the spot where the ball must be placed when a free-kick is being taken?

A. In the exact spot where the infraction occurred. All the offenses specified in the first part of Rule 12 are intended as committed on the precise spot where contact or attempted contact between players or by the hand touching the ball, if intentionally, has taken place. With regard to the so-called "distant offenses"—spitting at, throwing stones and other objects—as well as other cases of violent conduct and ungentlemanly conduct, the ball must be placed on the spot where the guilty player was standing at the time the offense was committed.

2. Q. Is it permitted to execute a free-kick when the ball is not completely stationary?

A. No. The moment the kick is taken, the ball must be stationary. Otherwise the free-kick must be retaken.

3. Q. Can a free-kick be taken backwards (kicking the ball toward own end)?

A. Yes, as long as the rule on how a free-kick taken by a defending team inside own penalty-area is fully observed.

4. Q. In which way must the referee indicate which free-kick he is assessing?

A. In the case of a direct free-kick, no particular signal is required. In the case of an indirect free-kick, the referee must give clear signal by raising the arm.

5. Q. In order to allow a teammate to execute a free-kick according to the rules, can a player hold the ball still with a hand or a foot to keep it from rolling because of strong winds?

   A. No. When, at the time play is resumed, because of strong winds the ball doesn't remain stationary on the ground, the referee must temporarily call the game. If the intensity of the wind does not abate and, thus, does not make possible a normal play, the game must definitely be suspended.

6. Q. In the case of a free-kick being taken, the ball placed nearest a touch-line or a goal-line leaves the playing field without first having covered the distance of 70 cm. (28 in.). What decision shall the referee take?

   A. The free-kick must be retaken.

7. Q. Can the player that executes the free-kick be allowed to cross over the touch-lines or the goal-lines in order to get a better run at the ball?

   A. Yes.

8. Q. Is it always required of opposing players to position themselves at the prescribed distance of 9.15 m. (10 yards) from the ball?

   A. Yes. The only exception being an indirect free-kick taken from inside the penalty-area at a distance from the defending goal which is less than 9.15 m. (10 yards). In such a case, the defending players can position themselves right on the goal-line. One must bear in mind that in all other cases a player taking a free-kick can disregard opposing players encroaching at a distance less than the required 9.15 m.; however in such an eventuality, if the ball is intercepted (by an opponent) the referee must not intervene.

9. Q. In the case of a free-kick being taken, can a player encroach in front of the ball in order to delay the game?

   A. No. The referee must immediately intervene to request the player encroaching near the ball to respect the prescribed distance (9.15 m.). In case of persistent delaying tactics, the player guilty of un-gentlemanly conduct shall be cautioned; if he further persists in delaying the game, he must be ejected from the game.

10. Q. Can an attacking player that has taken position beside or in the midst of a defending barrier (by defending players) duck down or move laterally in order not to intercept the ball kicked by a teammate (who has taken the free-kick)?

   A. Yes, as long as he does not commit any infractions to the rules of the game.

11. Q. When a free-kick is taken by a defending team from inside own penalty-area, can opposing players remain inside the same penalty-area?

A. No. It is required that they must position outside the penalty-area and keep the minimum distance from the ball of at least 9.15 m.

12. Q. When taking a free-kick from inside own penalty-area, can a goalie take the ball with his hands and then kick it?

A. No. The goalie must take the free-kick just as any other player. If he commits an infraction, the referee must act at once requesting to observe the rule, i.e., having the free-kick taken as required.

13. Q. A free-kick (direct or indirect) is taken by a defending team from inside the penalty-area. The ball crosses over the penalty-area, strikes a teammate and goes into own goal. Is the goal valid?

A. Yes.

14. Q. Can the player that has taken a free-kick play again the ball that has meantime covered the distance of 70 cm. (28 in.) but it has not been played by another player?

A. No. The infraction must be penalized with an indirect free-kick. One must bear in mind that if the ball bounces off the goal-posts, the corner-flag pole, the referee or a linesman who may at the moment be inside the playground, and is played again by the same player that took the free-kick, the infraction still exists. If the infraction occurs when the ball kicked from inside own penalty-area has not crossed the penalty-area markings, the free-kick must be retaken.

15. Q. In a free-kick situation, is the goal valid if the ball goes directly into own goal?

A. No. The goal is not valid whether scored on a direct or an indirect free-kick. In such an eventuality the play shall be resumed with a corner-kick. However if the free-kick has been taken from inside own penalty-area, it must be retaken.

16. Q. When taking an indirect free-kick, the ball is touched only by the player taking the free-kick. A teammate kicks the ball immediately and scores. Is the goal valid?

A. No. The rule requires that the ball must have traveled the minimum distance of 70 cm. in order to be considered played. Thus if the ball has only been touched, it is as if it has been kicked directly into goal by the second player; the play will then be resumed with a goal-kick. If the ball has been touched and slightly moved from its position but to a distance less than the required 70 cm. (28 in.), the free-kick must be retaken because the second player kicked the ball when the same was not yet in play.

17. Q. When, as a result of an indirect free-kick, the ball strikes an opponent and goes directly into goal, is the goal valid?

A. Yes.

18. Q. If a player that has taken the free-kick intentionally plays the ball with his hands but before it has been played by another player, must the referee punish the most serious foul, and in such a case, how?

A. Yes, by assessing a direct free-kick or a penalty-kick if the infraction occurred inside own penalty-area.

19. Q. Following the taking of a free-kick, a player ejected from the game plays the ball as he is leaving the field. What shall the referee do?

A. Such an eventuality should never occur, for the play must never resume until an ejected player has left the playground. Whenever such incident should occur because of the referee's carelessness, the free-kick must be retaken only after the ejected player has completely abandoned the playing field.

Cases on Law 14
"Penalty-Kick"

Chapter 17

1. Q. When a penalty-kick is being taken, what position should the players of both teams assume?

A. The player that takes the penalty-kick has the privilege to sprint away from the ball, either from inside or from outside the penalty-area. In the latter case, he must inform the referee that he is the kicker.

The defending goalie, from the moment the referee has whistled the taking of the penalty-kick and up until the ball is in play, i.e., has covered the required 70 cm. distance, must remain with his feet motionless on the goal-line and between the goal-posts. All the other players, defending or attacking ones, must remain inside the playing field but outside the penalty-area and at a distance of at least 9.15 m. (10 yards) from the penalty spot.

2. Q. If the players of the defending team persist in delaying the taking of a penalty-kick, what decision should the referee take?

A. First of all the referee must summon the captain of the team being penalized so that he can exhort his teammates to comply at once with the observance of the rules of the game. If the captain takes sides with his players, the referee must eject him from the game and invite the co-captain to urge the teammates to comply with the rules of the game. If even in this attempt the referee fails to assert his authority, he must leave the playing field and regard the game ended. In any case, the incident shall be reported in full details to the competent league or association.

3. Q. Is it necessary that, prior to the taking of a penalty-kick, the referee ascertain that all players have assumed the required position?

A. Yes. The referee must always make sure that all players take position in accordance with the rules.

4. Q. Can a player designated as the penalty kicker place the ball anywhere other than the penalty spot because of poor ground conditions?

A. No.

5. Q. The penalty kicker darts away, fakes the shot (to kick the ball) in a certain way, and then kicks the ball in a different way. Is such a move allowed in order to deceive the opposing goalie?

A. Yes. The penalty-shot kicker can fake the shot in any way in order to deceive the goalie, as long as such deception is immediate between the sprint and the shot. However such tactics are not allowed if the kicker stops while running at the ball in order to induce the goalie to move one direction, and subsequently kicks the ball in the opposite direction. Such action is contrary to the spirit of fair play; the player guilty of such an act must be cautioned, and if a goal has resulted the penalty-kick must be retaken.

6. Q. Is a penalty-kick valid if taken before the referee has whistled?

A. No. The penalty-kick must be retaken, irrespective of the outcome.

7. Q. At the moment the referee blows the whistle to signal the taking of the penalty-kick, another player other than the recognized kicker kicks the ball and scores. Is the goal valid?

A. No. Such action is contrary to the spirit of the game. Thus the referee shall disallow the goal, shall caution both players guilty of misconduct and shall order the penalty-kick retaken. In the event the ball has crossed the goal-line, outside the goal-posts, or above the cross-bar, the play shall resume with a goal-kick and the guilty players dealt the required disciplinary sanctions.

8. Q. The player kicking a penalty passes the ball backward to a teammate who scores. Is the goal valid?

A. No. The goal must be disallowed and the penalty-kick retaken.

9. Q. If a player intentionally takes position outside the boundary lines (outside the playing field) when a penalty shot is being taken, should the referee caution him and, if he persists, should the referee eject him?

A. Yes.

10. Q. Can there be off-side when a penalty shot is being taken?

A. Yes, whenever the ball, instead of being kicked forward (toward the goal), is rather passed to a teammate whose position at the time the penalty-kick is being taken is in front of the penalty spot. It is significant to recall at this point that if the ball bounces off a goal-post or the cross-bar and goes to a teammate (of the kicker), it is as if the ball had been passed directly from one player (the kicker) to another; vice-versa, if the ball is kicked directly into a goal and a score results, this is a valid goal, even though one or more teammates of the kicker were off-side but outside the penalty-area and, therefore, at the required distance from the ball; in this specific instance, the off-side is not punishable.

11. Q. The ball bounces off a goal-post or the cross-bar (of the goal) and returns to the penalty-kicker who plays the ball again. Is this play normal?

A. No. The penalty-kicker has played the ball twice in a resumption of play; he must, therefore, be penalized with an indirect free-kick.

12. Q. The player assigned to take the penalty shot waits for the referee to give the signal with the whistle. Suddenly a defending player kicks the ball into his own goal and scores. What decision should the referee take?

A. The referee shall disallow the goal, shall caution the player who has committed the infraction and shall have the penalty-kick retaken according to the rules. Of course, in addition to the caution to be administered, the penalty shot must be taken by an attacking player, even though a goal may have not resulted.

13. Q. If the penalty shot is retaken because of any one violation of the rules, should it be taken by the same player or by a different player (of the attacking team)?

A. A penalty-kick can be retaken by a player other than the one who did originally take the first shot, as long as the referee is informed in advance as to the identity of the selected kicker who may then take a run at the ball from outside the penalty area.

14. Q. Can a penalty-kicker pass the ball forward to a teammate who quickly shoots and scores?

A. Yes, provided that:
   a. all players, except the one taking the penalty shot and the goalkeeper, were standing outside the penalty-area and at a distance from the penalty-spot of at least 9.15 m. (10 yds.) the exact moment the kick was taken;
   b. the player to whom the ball was passed by the penalty-kicker was not off-side at the exact moment the ball was kicked;
   c. the penalty-kick is being taken while the game is in progress and the requirements of the law (14) are abided by.

15. Q. Following the referee's signal (by his whistle) to the penalty-kicker to proceed, but just before the ball has been played, an attacking player enters the penalty-area. A goal is scored. Is the goal valid?

   A. No. The referee shall disallow the goal, caution the player that has committed the infraction and order the penalty-kick retaken.

16. Q. In the same circumstances as outlined above (15), the player who has committed the infraction to the rule takes control of the ball which has been cleared by the goalkeeper or bounced off a goal-post or the cross-bar, and scores a goal. What shall the referee do?

   A. He shall disallow the goal, caution the guilty player, and resume the play with an indirect free-kick against the attacking team.

17. Q. The same infraction as outlined above (15 and 16) has been committed by a defending player. What decision shall the referee take?

   A. If a goal has resulted, it is valid. If the ball has crossed the goal-line or has been stopped and cleared by the goalkeeper, or bounced off a goal-post or the cross-bar, the penalty-kick must be retaken. In any case, the guilty player must be cautioned.

18. Q. If several players of both teams simultaneously enter the penalty-area or encroach at a distance from the ball that is less than the required 9.15 m., but just before the ball is in play, what decision shall the referee take?

   A. He shall caution all the players guilty of the infraction and order the penalty-kick to be retaken, regardless of the outcome of the preceding kick.

19. Q. In attempting to upset the penalty-kicker, a defending player starts to make fun of, screams, or throws an object. What shall the referee do?

   A. If a goal has resulted in the meantime, it is valid. If no goal has resulted, the penalty-kick shall be retaken. As far as disciplinary actions are concerned, the referee shall caution the player guilty of ungentlemanly conduct, or shall eject him from the game if in his judgment the object was thrown with the specific intent of injuring the opposing player.

20. Q. As a protest against the referee who has assessed a penalty-kick against the defending team, the goalkeeper refuses to take position as set forth by the rules, or even leaves the field of play, what shall the referee do?

   A. He shall eject or consider ejected the protesting goalkeeper. Then he shall summon the captain of the defending team and request the substitution of the goalkeeper with one of the players already on the field.

21. **Q.** After a goal has been scored on a penalty-kick, the captain of the team that has suffered the goal makes formal, verbal reservations regarding the distance between the penalty-spot and the goal-line as being allegedly irregular. Are such complaints (reservations) valid?

   A. Verbal complaints may be made and the referee should take notice in the presence of the captain of the opposing team, so long as there are irregularities which may occur on the field of play in the course of a match. In the case in point, since the complaint concerns one part of the markings of the playground, unchanged in the course of the game, the same reservations (complaints) should have been made in writing prior to the start of the game. In any case, the referee is always required to note in his report the reservations expressed (lodged to him).

22. **Q.** During the taking of a penalty-kick assessed at the end of the official time, the defending goalie commits an infraction and immediately afterward even the penalty-kicker, or another forward, commits an infringement to the law. What decision should the referee take?

   A. He must first of all take into consideration the infraction committed by the goalkeeper, because it occurred first; he shall have the penalty-kick retaken and then caution both players.

23. **Q.** If the penalty-kick is taken or retaken at the expiration of the normal period, at what moment should the referee call the end of the playing half?

   A. As soon as the trajectory of the ball has concluded any one phase of a play. For more detailed explanations, refer to Law 14.

24. **Q.** At the moment the penalty-kick is taken, the ball deflates or becomes irregular during the trajectory. What should the referee do?

   A. Since the ball was normal at the time it was placed on the penalty spot it must be assumed the irregularity has occurred as a result of the kick. Thus the penalty-kick must be retaken.

25. **Q.** What decision should the referee take if, following the taking of a penalty shot, the ball hits a goal-post or the cross-bar and bursts?

   A. The referee shall resume the play with a new ball and drop the same. One must bear in mind, however, that if the penalty-kick has been taken at the expiration of the normal period and the ball hits a goal-post or the cross-bar, the playing period ends the moment the ball is kicked.

26. **Q.** When a penalty kick is taken, the trajectory of the ball is altered by a foreign object or anything extraneous to the game. What shall the referee do?

   A. He must order the penalty-kick retaken.

Cases on Law 15
"Throw-In"

Chapter 18

1. Q. If a player, while throwing the ball in from a side-line, thrusts the same in such a way that it doesn't enter the playing field, what decision should the referee make?

A. He shall order the throw-in retaken (by the same team).

2. Q. Can the player that executes the throw-in from the side-line throw the ball with full force into the field of play?

A. Yes, as long as the ball comes from behind and above the head.

3. Q. When should the throw-in from the side-lines be considered improper, and what decisions should the referee make in such circumstances?

A. The throw-in from the side-line is improper when the player that executes it:

a. doesn't face the playground;

b. doesn't keep at least one portion of each foot on the ground, outside the touch-line, or touching the same; (see Diagram 35, p. 186);

c. doesn't throw the ball from behind the head and doesn't release it above the head;

d. drops instead of throwing the ball;

e. actually throws the ball with one hand and directs it with the other.

When the throw-in is taken improperly, the referee must have it retaken by the opposing team on the same spot.

If the player that executes the throw-in takes position on a spot which is higher or lower than the level of the playing field, the throw-in must be retaken by the same team.

4. Q. If the throw-in by the other team is also improper, what shall the referee do?

A. He shall have the first team repeat the throw-in again.

5. Q. In what way should the referee stop the persistent infractions to Law 15?

A. After the second consecutive infraction the referee shall caution the player that has executed the throw-in as well as his captain in order to establish the team liability. Then he will have the other team take the throw-in again. At the third consecutive infraction the referee shall eject the player guilty of the new infraction and assign the throw-in to the other team. When further infractions occur consecutively the referee shall regard the persistent infractions of Law 15 as ungentlemanly behavior intended to obstruct the game by both teams, and shall call the game for good.

6. Q. What is the reason the infractions committed when the throw-in is taken are not technically punishable?

A. Because they occur when the ball is out of play.

7. Q. Can the throw-in be taken by a goalkeeper?

A. Yes.

8. Q. If the player that executes the throw-in doesn't touch the touch-line with his feet, must he take position at a certain distance from the same?

A. No. One must be advised, however, that the throw-in must always be taken from the purpose-field area which is 1.50 m. in width.

9. Q. When a player executes the throw-in from a side-line, are opposing players required to stand at a certain distance?

A. No. Opponents must stand inside the field of play, at any distance, as long as they cause no inconvenience to the player taking the throw-in. Whenever a player dances about or gesticulates to distract or impede the thrower, he shall be cautioned for ungentlemanly conduct.

10. Q. Can the throw-in from the side-line be taken while running?

A. No, for it is required that at least a portion of each foot must be in contact with the ground (at the time the ball is released).

11. Q. Can the throw-in from the side-line be taken by standing with the legs spread apart?

A. Yes.

12. Q. Can the ball be played immediately after being thrown-in regularly, or is it necessary to wait until the ball covers the ground at least the distance equal to its circumference?

A. The law makes quite clear that the ball is in play as soon as it has crossed the touch-line, and, therefore, can be played immediately without waiting for it to cover any distance.

13. Q. Can the thrower intentionally send the ball into an area other than the field of play?

A. No. When such eventuality occurs, the referee shall caution the player and order the throw-in retaken by the same team.

14. Q. Is there off-side when a throw-in from the side-line is taken?

A. No. A player that receives the ball directly from a teammate that has taken the throw-in from the side-line is never off-side.

15. Q. When executing a throw-in from the side-line, is it allowed to hit an opponent with the ball?

A. Yes, but only if the ball is thrown without deliberate force and with the evident intent of getting it back. However, whenever the ball is thrown with violent intent, the guilty player must at once be ejected from the game for violent conduct. In such instance the play shall be resumed:
a. with an indirect free-kick from the spot where the throw-in was taken, if the guilty player has thrown the ball standing on the side-line with at least a portion of each foot;
b. with a throw-in from the side-line by the same team if the guilty player has thrown the ball from well outside the touch-line.

16. Q. If a player who is executing the throw-in from the side-line intentionally throws the ball at the referee, what punishment shall be assessed?

A. The referee shall eject the player guilty of violent conduct. The play shall resume as by #15, Law 15.

17. Q. Following a normal throw-in from a side-line, the ball accidentally touches the referee, or a linesman (standing just inside the field of play), the corner flag-post or a goal-post and goes directly:
a. into a goal;
b. beyond a touch-line;
c. beyond a goal-line, but outside the goal-posts.
In what way must the play be resumed?

A. a. with a corner-kick if the ball has entered into the goal of the player that has taken the throw-in; with a goal-kick if the ball has entered into the opponents' goal;
b. with a new throw-in by the opposing team if the ball has gone out of the touch-line;
c. with a corner-kick if the ball has crossed the goal-line of the thrower; with a goal-kick if the ball has crossed the opposing goal-line (no goal).

18. Q. After taking the throw-in from the side-line normally as required by the rule, a player plays the ball again before it has been played (touched) by another player, or intentionally plays it again with the hand. What decision shall the referee take?

A. In the first instance, he shall assess an indirect free-kick; in the second instance, a direct free-kick. Both free-kicks must be taken from the spot where the infraction was committed.

Cases on Law 16
"Goal-Kick"

Chapter 19

1. Q. In what way should one interpret the provision concerning the taking of a goal-kick by which the ball "shall be placed on any point within that half of the goal-area nearest to where it crossed the line"?

A. By "half of the goal-area," it is meant that portion which results by drawing an imaginary line from the center of the goal-line to the center of the parallel line marking the larger side of the goal-area. By the above, it is clear that the ball doesn't have to be necessarily placed at the corner formed by the lines marking the goal-area inward to the playing field.

In the eventuality the ball has gone outside the playing field after crossing the goal-line above the cross-bar right at its center, the goal-kick can be taken equally from either half of the goal-area but always upon the referee's directions.

2. Q. In order to take the goal-kick, is it necessary that the ball be placed entirely inside the goal-area?

A. No. It is enough that only a portion of the ball be placed on a line limiting the goal-area.

3. Q. When is the ball considered in play following a goal-kick?

A. When it has entirely crossed a line marking the penalty-area inside the playing field.

4. Q. Can the opposing players remain inside the penalty-area when a goal-kick is taken?

A. No. As long as the ball has not crossed the penalty-area, the opposing players must take position outside the penalty-area. If a player violates this rule, he must be warned and, if habitual offender (recidivist), he must be cautioned.

5. Q. The goal-kick has been taken. A player, defenseman, or forward, touches the ball before it has left the penalty-area. What shall the referee do?

A. He will have the goal-kick retaken, for the infraction has occurred when the ball was not yet in play. If a player commits a second infraction, he must be cautioned and if he still persists in infringing the laws of the game he must be ejected from the game.

6. Q. The player that has taken the goal-kick intentionally touches the ball with the hand right outside the penalty-area, but before it has been played by another player. What decision shall the referee take?

A. He shall assess a direct free-kick in favor of the opposing team.

7. Q. A player other than the goalkeeper takes a goal-kick. The ball travels outside the penalty-area but comes back into the penalty-area repelled back by a strong wind before any other player has touched it. A defenseman, other than the goalkeeper, plays the ball with the hand inside the penalty area. Should the referee assess a penalty-kick?

A. Yes. If, in a similar case, the goal-keeper takes the goal-kick and tries to grab the ball which nonetheless rolls into goal, the referee shall assess an indirect free-kick.

8. Q. A goal-kick is taken; the ball covers a distance equal to its circumference while an opposing player runs inside the penalty-area and is intentionally fouled by a defenseman. Can a penalty-kick be assessed?

A. No, for at the moment the foul was committed the ball was not in play. The guilty player must nonetheless be cautioned or ejected from the game, depending upon the kind of foul committed, and the goal-kick must be retaken.

9. Q. While a goal-kick is being taken, a player intentionally trips an opponent before the ball runs outside the penalty-area. Should the referee assess a free-kick?

A. No. The ball is not considered in play before it has run outside the penalty-area. Consequently the guilty player must be cautioned, or ejected if the seriousness of the foul warrants it, while the goal-kick must be retaken.

10. Q. Is there off-side when a goal-kick is taken?

A. No. Law 11 clearly states that there is never off-side on a goal-kick.

11. Q. While taking a goal-kick a player sends the ball beyond his own goal-line, through the space marking the penalty-area. Should a corner-kick be assessed?

A. No. The ball has not left the penalty-area inside the field of play, consequently the goal-kick must be retaken. If, however, the ball crosses over the goal-line in the area not limited by the penalty-area (outside), a corner-kick must be assessed.

12. Q. On a goal-kick, after leaving the penalty-area the ball goes into goal, directly or after striking the referee. Is the goal valid?

A. No. The law clearly states that on a goal-kick a goal cannot be scored directly. Thus, if such eventuality occurs the play must be resumed:
a. with a corner-kick if the ball has crossed into the goal of the team that took the goal-kick;
b. with a goal-kick if the ball ran into the opponents' goal.

Cases on Law 17
"Corner-Kick"

Chapter 20

1. Q. A ball played by a defenseman strikes the referee or a linesman (just inside the field of play), or the corner flag-post and goes into goal. How should the play be resumed?

A. With a corner-kick.

2. Q. Is a corner-kick regarded a free-kick?

A. No. It is a resumption of play which does not follow an infraction.

3. Q. In order for a corner-kick to be taken, can the ball be placed right on a line marking the corner-area?

A. Yes, for the perimetral lines (touch-lines and goal-lines) as well as the arc marking the corner-area are all part of the game.

4. Q. When a corner-kick is being taken, are the players required to take certain positions on the field of .play?

A. All players of the defending team must take position at a distance not less than 9.15 m. (10 yards) from the ball until the same has been played. Conversely, the players of the attacking team can take any position.

5. Q. Is there off-side on a corner-kick?

A. No. A player that receives the ball directly on a corner-kick is never off-side. However, this exception to Law 11 becomes invalid as soon as the ball, having been played according to the rules, is touched by another forward player. One must bear in mind that if the player that has taken the corner-kick quickly takes position not in conflict with Law 11 before a teammate plays the ball, his new position is perfectly regular.

6. Q. Can the corner-flag be removed in order to better execute the corner-kick?

A. No. Such being an infraction, the guilty player must be cautioned and if he persists he must at once be ejected from the game.

7. Q. Can a goal be scored directly on a corner-kick?

A. Yes, it can; not only against the opponents, but theoretically even against own goal.

8. Q. If, following a corner-kick the ball bounces off a goal-post, touches the referee or a linesman inside the playing field, and comes back to the corner-kicker, can he play the ball a second time?

A. No. The player that has taken the corner-kick cannot play the ball a second time unless the same has been first played by another player. If this rule is infringed, an indirect free-kick shall be assessed on behalf of the opposing team.

9. Q. On a corner-kick the ball crosses over the goal-line during the trajectory and then lands inside the field of play. What shall the referee do?

A. He shall assess a goal-kick, for the ball ceased to be in play the moment it crossed the goal-line in flight.

10. Q. On a corner-kick the ball crosses over the goal-line but before covering a distance equal to its circumference. What shall the referee do?

A. He must order the corner-kick retaken, for the ball was not in play when it crossed the goal-line.

11. Q. On a corner-kick, can a player take position in front of the opposing goalie in order to obstruct his view of the ball or his movements?

A. Provided all players of the defending team must take position at a distance of at least 9.15 m (10 yards) from the ball, each player can take any position he finds convenient. However, when not playing the ball, it is against Rule 12 to intentionally obstruct an opponent. This is more so in the case of obstructing the goalie who is not in possession of the ball.

12. Q. On a corner-kick while the ball is in its trajectory after being kicked, the defending goalie is charged by a forward (opponent) and falls inside the goal. What decision shall the referee take?

A. If the charge is a fair one, the referee shall assess an indirect free-kick, for the goalkeeper was charged inside his own goal-area while he was not in possession of the ball and was not obstructing an opponent within playing range of the ball. However, if the charge was not a fair one, i.e., violent, dangerous, or brutal, the referee shall punish the attacking team with a direct free-kick. The technical sanction doesn't bar further disciplinary actions as the case may require.

PART THREE

Conduct of Referees

Chapter 21

Any referee appointed to officiate a match is in full charge as well as the sole timekeeper. Also he is the sole judge whose decision is final in all questions pertaining to any facts relative to the game. He is also the reporter of any incidents that may have occurred before, during, and after the game. A referee is the official representative of organized soccer on the playing field to players, club officials, and spectators.

It is obvious, thus, that in performing his difficult duties the referee must be the true expression of uprightness, impartiality, and very high regard for sportsmanship, for he must make sure, by enforcing intelligently and logically the true spirit of the laws of the game that the match be played in a natural fashion. In order to achieve such goal in the best possible way, he must be serenely and physically well prepared; he must always be updated in the knowledge of all rules which control the game. In other words, with his deportment he must display all the requisites accruing to the dignity and qualification of a "game official." Any regulations pertaining to the uniform, the same for all referees of any categories, are periodically issued by the ruling body of the Referee Association.

Duties of Referees, Before, During, and After the Game

Chapter22

The referee should have with him a special notecard or notebook on which he should annotate:

> a. the starting time;
>
> b. the ending time of each period;
>
> c. the team that took the kick-off;
>
> d. the time a goal was scored and the name of the player, and team, that did the scoring;
>
> e. the number of players' jerseys (to help in the identification) who were substituted, cautioned, or ejected;
>
> f. the precise time the incident(s) occurred;
>
> g. the minutes wasted and recuperated at the end of each period; and
>
> h. the time the game was called off.

Before the Game

The referee assigned to a game should reach the place where the game is to be played well ahead of time in order to be in the best physical condition. In any case, if using public transportation, he should never rely on the last run which would bring him on the field of play at the last minute. Official regulations on the matter should, as they do in most cases, spell out all the normal procedures the referee should follow. He should plan to be at his destination at least forty-five minutes prior to the scheduled starting time, so that he has sufficient time, first to closely inspect the field-of-play's readiness; to put on his uniform; to carry out and complete all the preliminaries (check the players' identities), then walk into the field and whistle the start of the match exactly on time.

When he arrives in the dressroom assigned to the officials, the referee should examine its entire setup and report to the competent league or association any possible lack of basic facilities which do not respond to athletic needs. As soon as he has put on his uniform, he should request the club official** assigned to him to supply the completed lineups (two copies) of the names of the players in each team, including the substitutes and all persons authorized to remain close to the playground during the game. The lineups, which must be signed by the club official(s) assigned to the referee, should be handed to the referee along with the pass-cards or any other official identification cards for each player, club official, coach, trainer, or even the doctor.

The referee should carefully make sure that the names and numbers of the players' pass-cards correspond to those listed on the lineups. He has authority to allow any player to participate in a match even though no official pass-card can be produced. In this case, the player in question can be allowed to play but only if the club official assigned to the referee files with the official a written statement claiming that the position of the player in relation to the club is legitimate. At the same time, the player in question must be able to provide an official document, with photograph for identification, issued by a government agency or the like. A driving license or the card issued by the Immigration and Naturalization Service are most desirable. The number on the jersey must be identical to the one that appears on the lineup beside the name of the player, starting or substitute. After checking the identities of the players (a team at a time to avoid confusion), the referee shall check the regularity of the balls provided for the match which must be available at all times for the duration of the game. The referee then will deliver one of the two lineups (provided by each team) to the official, or the captain, of the opposing team. In some cases, quite frequently indeed in Europe, the referee is required by the league to receive a certain amount of money the home team must produce prior to the starting time. In the United States, namely in the local league games, the home club must pay the referee an agreed sum of money due for traveling expenses and other commitments before the start of the game.

After all the preliminaries have been exhausted, the referee will enter the field of play along with the linesmen and all the starting players and will take position in the middle of the playing field to salute the public. He will then quickly inspect the nets (if no official linesmen are present) to see that they are fixed properly, the corner flags and the markings on the playing field. Subsequently he shall drop the coin on the ground for the choice of the field or of the kick-off by giving priority to the captain of the visiting team. Having fulfilled this last duty, the referee is now ready to blow the whistle and start the game as by the rules.

**In order to provide protection and safety for the person of the referee, the home team should assign, as it is customary in most countries, at least one club official to assist the referee in anything he may need from the time he reaches the location. His cooperation must be complete and fully supportive in case of incidents on the field or outside.

During the Game

The referee shall avoid:

    a. an exceedingly authoritarian attitude;

    b. to manifest his decisions with theatrical gesticulations;

    c. to call the fouls and the infractions too late, seemingly, as too frequently occurs after the protests both of spectators and players;

    d. to blow the whistle repeatedly and in a rather prolonged fashion, particularly when there is no justifiable reason for it;

    e. to appear hesitant and nervous;

    f. to argue with the players;

    g. to explain and justify his decisions;

    h. to call the attention of players by pointing at them or touching them in any way or for any reason;

    i. to cause unnecessary delays, e.g., by correcting the position of the ball before taking a free-kick;

    j. to run, jump, and move in a way not consonant to a serious individual actively involved in sports;

    k. to stand still on the playground while the game is in progress, or with the hands on his hips as if indicating off-side the same as in American football;

    l. to take position which interferes with the progress of the game;

    m. to compel a player to retrieve the ball he kicked away as a protest or because of a deliberate attempt to waste time;

    n. voluntary time-wasting at any start of play, by cautioning or ejecting a player, if a repeated offender, that deliberately delays the resumption of play.

The referee must keep in mind that as a rule, when he blows the whistle he intends to stop a play as well as restart it.

The referee must always display:

    a. a courteous, dignified, and subdued demeanor toward players; club officials; and other individuals as well;

    b. timeliness every time he intervenes, though applying intelligently the "advantage clause." The "advantage" can best be applied if the referee restrains from constantly holding the whistle in his mouth;

    c. ability to control the taking of corner-kicks, goal-kicks, free-kicks, throw-ins (from the side-lines);

    d. awareness of the efficient and constant effort by the linesmen;

    e. sense of superior, dignified personality when dealing with anyone;

    f. ability to enforce the laws of the game (and all the regulations issued by the competent association, national or international), constantly and coherently for the entire duration of the match, irrespective of the importance or relevance of the match itself and wherever the same is played;

g. firmness in the performance of his duties, peace of mind, gentlemanliness, and high sense of sportsmanship;

h. full knowledge and understanding of the laws of the game and to enforce them with simplicity of manners;

i. perfect physical conditions and sufficient stamina to follow the play very closely for the duration of the game;

j. quick reflexes in all situations;

k. ability to attract notice the least possible;

l. indifference to insults and threats coming from spectators;

m. speaking effectiveness and conciseness when strictly necessary;

n. ability to perform effectively irrespective of the nature and importance of the match, keeping in mind that his duty is not to punish but to play; to make sure that everything conforms to the rules;

o. ability to make, at the right time and with the necessary firmness, all decisions whether technical or disciplinary, as required by the laws of the game in order to keep away from the field violence, intimidation, ungentlemanly conduct, brutality, and the like;

p. to use, whenever possible, all the available means to bring the match to an end and to avoid, if at all possible, suspending the game;

q. to extend his control beyond the playing field, i.e., to the entire sports complex.

It is advisable that the referee:

a. take position near the midfield, laterally to the circle, facing the side toward which the kick-off is being taken to make sure that everything conforms to the rules regarding the start of play (see Diagram 3, p. 151);

b. take position on the portion of the goal-area opposite to the corner where the corner-kick is being taken. In this way it is possible to observe the players without interfering with their play;

c. take position around the midfield when a goal-kick is being taken so that he will not find himself cut off by subsequent play developments, making sure that the goal-kick is taken properly;

d. take position on a throw-in closer to the zone where the ball may reasonably be thrown so that he may follow further developments of play;

e. move quickly, on a free-kick, without losing control of the modalities of resumption of play, toward the zone where the ball will seemingly be kicked, but avoiding interference with the trajectory of the ball;

f. take position on a penalty-kick on the lower portion of one of the sides of the goal-area, on a point which ideally parallels the penalty-spot, facing the linesman (if an official one) who will have taken the position on the opposite side, on the spot marked by the goal-line merging the goal area;

g. make sure to be always facing the zone where the action is or where the resumption of play has been taken from;

h. never stand or run against the sun;

i. never follow the trajectory of the ball, when, after being kicked very high is about to drop on the field of play, for precisely those brief moments many fouls involving players occur;

j. lift the right arm to indicate an indirect free-kick (to distinguish this from the direct free-kick which does not require any signal). (See referee's duties.)

After the Game

The referee normally leaves the field of play following all the players of the visiting team but followed by the home team. In such way it is possible to observe the behavior both of the players and of the club officials. Inside the dressroom, and afterward, he must avoid making statements concerning the match already played or expressing opinions or judgments concerning facts, circumstances, or persons having any bearing to the game; be mindful to report any incidents to the competent league and the Referee Association. Whenever the need arises, he shall request the intervention of the home team's officials in order to secure his personal safety as well as that of the linesmen, of the players, and official of the visiting team; always keeping a dignified and serene deportment. He shall thereafter prepare the official report and send it, as by prior instruction, to the competent league or association.

Collaboration Between Referee and Linesmen

Chapter 23

All the instructions outlined herein constitute the procedure that all referees must follow in order to practically and effectively enforce all rules and regulations set forth by the F.I.F.A. as well as those of the national or local associations. It must be emphasized once more that ... "The referee is the sole judge whose decisions are final in all points of fact connected with the play, so far as the outcome of the game is concerned." Linesmen are his collaborators. It follows that the duty of the linesmen is one of cooperation with the referee in the manner and limits set forth by him in advance of the match, keeping in mind that only he possesses discretionary powers to decide all disputes and judge facts, technical and disciplinary, which occur in the course of a game. The referee, thus, as a general rule is not required to make decisions as a result of a linesman's signal when he himself has closely observed the fact that has determined the linesman to signal. Nonetheless, when the linesmen are officially appointed to assist the referee, if he consults one of them for any clarification concerning a fact which escaped his scrutiny, in part or entirely, he must then accept the linesman's version and reach, consequently, his final decision.

The official rules set forth by F.I.F.A. and the American Federation (U.S.S.A.) clearly state that the referee cannot ignore the cooperation of the linesmen provided by the clubs in order to avail himself of that of colleagues present at the game but not officially designated.

So far as assignment of a referee, his substitution (in case of absence or unavailability is concerned), all decisions by the U.S.S.A. are to be abided by.

It must be made clear at this point that:
>   a. the names of the linesmen assigned by the clubs must be
>   included in official lineups along with those of the players and

other club officials authorized to stand within the boundaries of the playing field;

b. the club linesmen do not need to be registered as players but be identified by an accepted I.D. document (as described above); but if they are registered players they must be at least sixteen years old, unless the match involves teams of a youth league, in which case the minimum age is the universally accepted one of fourteen years old;

c. if no club linesmen have been made available, the referee can request, but not demand, that players from the roster be assigned to perform the duties of linesmen;

d. a player who has started the game as a linesman cannot subsequently interrupt such duty in order to take part in the game;

e. two linesmen must be present for the duration and completion of a game.

Instructions to Linesmen

Chapter 24

In order to obtain the best possible cooperation among the three officials, all matters affecting their cooperation should be fully discussed prior to the game, and the referee should issue his instructions clearly and distinctly. He should give instructions as indicated below:

a. *to the club linesmen:*

He shall make quite clear that, no matter what their opinions on any facts may be, his decision is final and irrevocable. He will further make clear that their duty is to signal only when the ball has completely crossed the touch-lines or the goal-lines. The referee has the final say as to which side shall take the throw-in or whether a corner-kick should be awarded.

b. *to the official linesmen:*

Since they are expressly appointed by the Referee Association, or the like, hence they are colleagues, the referee can assign to them more duties in order to achieve a more valid cooperation and a more effective control of the game and anything concerning the same. The referee, then, shall indicate to his collaborators right before the game:

1. the time marked on his watch (thus all three officials will have their watches synchronized);

2. who the senior linesman is (he shall carry the red flag to designate senior status);

3. which half field each linesman should operate, preferably left wing first half and right wing second half, with the referee on a diagonal to suit, so that all four corners of the playing field are adequately covered, and

so that all players come under the referee's direct supervision at some stage of the game (see Diagram 2, p. 150);

4. the method he will follow in the progress of the game, how he will move from a certain position to another on a given circumstance or as the field conditions will warrant;

5. which duties the linesmen should perform prior to the start of the game, such as checking the playing conditions of the field, the markings of the playing field, the goals, the nets (if they are properly attached to the posts, the cross-bar, and the ground), the corner flags and whatever other aspect of the field or equipment used in the game as the referee may request;

6. that they (the three of them) are properly equipped with whistle, pencil, notebook, coin, and two watches, one with stop action. The senior linesman should take time out on his stop watch whenever the referee indicates time out, so that he has the official time personally if needed.

7. which signals should be used during the game (a standard set of signals will normally operate in all games and all officials should be familiar with them): when the ball has entirely crossed the side lines or the goal lines between the goal-posts, when a corner kick is awarded, which side shall be entitled to take the throw-in, when there is off-side.

8. which duties should be observed at any resumption of play;

9. how he will acknowledge the signal if he has perceived it, and how he will, in his judgment, decide not to stop the play.

During the Game

Aside from its strictly technical nature, in relation to the match, the cooperation by the official linesmen is of great importance particularly when disciplinary action is called. As a matter of fact, cases of brutal or violent conduct by players are not infrequent when the attention of the referee is directed to a portion of the playing field opposite to the one where deplorable acts may occur. In such cases, the linesman shall call the referee's attention by agitating the flag as required, reporting to the referee, who has meanwhile stopped the play, that a player has intentionally struck an opponent or the same linesman before the play was stopped. The referee will then take both technical as well as disciplinary action, as the case shall require. However, whenever the violent or brutal acts have preceded playing action (ejection of the culprit), he shall resume play by dropping the ball on the spot where it was at the time the play was stopped.

The referee will definitely refrain from consulting a linesman when technical and disciplinary acts occurred before his own eyes (when he had full control of the acts). If he did so, he would clearly show to unload upon his linesman any responsibility for judging the facts, which would constitute an unforgivable infraction of the referee's moral ethics.

What the referee has observed, even imperfectly, ought to be instead verified and evaluated after the play has been stopped, with the valid help of the linesman closer to the play who will, then, be consulted.

In any case, the referee shall avoid consulting with the linesman if pressingly and persistently requested by the players or, worse still, by intimidations by the same. The referee shall also refrain from assigning to the linesmen duties which actually imply some form of officiating, even though such decision might be considered appropriate or even desirable in certain circumstances. The referee shall never display, in any uncertain terms, any intentions when players and spectators as well are violently disagreeing with his decisions, which would make it appear his decision was reached as a result of the linesman's signal.

After the Game

The referee has the obligation to accept any statements given by the linesmen relative to violent or brutal behavior by players or other personnel authorized to stay close to the playing field, not only at the end of the first half but also at the conclusion of the match, when such violent or brutal acts have escaped the referee's direct control. The linesman's statements must be written and given to the referee who will then forward them, along with his own report, to the competent league or association, which will then have the duty to judge the facts and take the necessary disciplinary actions.

All these formalities must be observed in absolute privacy, i.e., without the presence of club officials, players, or other individuals including other referees who may be present at the game. Whenever necessary the referee shall always support the actions as well as the prestige of his linesmen.

Duties of Linesmen

Chapter 25

Unless requested otherwise by the referee, the official linesmen should abide by the following procedure:

Before the Game

1. to appear on the playground, possibly along with the referee, at least forty-five minutes prior to the official start of the game;
2. to diligently follow the instructions, preliminary to the game, spelled out by the referee;
3. to ascertain that the official flags are in proper order, i.e., one red and the other yellow. If the playing field is covered with snow, the color of the flags must be clearly distinguishable from white;
4. to check the goals and nets, as well as the corner flags;
5. to synchronize their own watches with the referee's.

During the Game

1. to control the half of the playground as indicated by the referee;
2. to follow closely all aspects of play which develop inside the half field assigned to his supervision; in such way, he can judge, upon the referee's request, precisely and objectively, any facts which have taken place;
3. to give a timely signal when the ball has entirely crossed the side-line or the goal-line, indicating then which team shall be entitled to resume play, if either a goal-kick or a corner-kick should be assessed. However

in all those facts which the referee has directly and closely observed and, therefore, able to make a decision by himself the linesman must refrain from giving any signal;

4. to timely signal, but not persistently (by holding the flag high for quite some time) all off-sides. In order to signal off-sides, the linesman must keep in mind that the signaling of an irregular position by a player must be immediate, but in order to call the attention of the referee with his flag it is necessary that such players directly intervene in the play or actively interfere with the opponents' play. In other words, while the off-side position must be detected only the moment a teammate of the player in off-side position plays the ball, it is advisable to avoid untimely interventions, for the player in off-side may not clearly and actively be participating in the play;

5. to signal immediately, by taking position in the best possible spot in order to be seen by the referee by agitating the flag persistently, that a player has, while the referee is following the play in another area of the playing field, committed violent or brutal acts against an opponent or the same linesman. Whenever the referee cannot, from his position, detect the linesman's signaling, the other linesman must call the referee's attention by using his flag the same way until one of the two signals has been detected by the referee who shall at once stop the play.

   It must be pointed out, however, that the simple attempt to strike an opponent does not call for any signaling by the linesman.

6. to signal all players who enter or re-enter the field of play while the ball is in play, without the referee's prior assent;

7. to provide, upon the referee's request, any verbal reservations presented by the captain (of one team) regarding the measurements of the playing field or its regularity, as well as a refusal-in-writing to continue to play the game;

8. to offer the referee, whenever he requests them, any clarifications regarding the time elapsed or the minutes left to play before the end of either half time as well as those minutes wasted as a result of pro-longed delays or interruptions primarily caused by injuries or other serious causes.

Since the linesmen's duties are to assist and help the referee but not one of interference or opposition to the referee, the linesmen must always make sure, before signaling any infraction, that the referee may be in a better position to perceive and judge an infraction to the rules. Furthermore they must avoid any intervention inside the field of play unless expressly requested to do so by the referee.

Linesmen are not to retrieve the ball that has rolled across the side-lines or goal-lines; they must make sure that the goal-kick, the throw-in and the corner-kick are taken in accordance with the rules. In order to better observe the above resumptions of play, they must take the following positions:

    a. on a goal-kick in line with the ball (to see if it is properly placed);

    b. on a throw-in—near the player who takes it;

    c. on a corner-kick—beyond the goal-line, as indicated by the referee (normally by the goal-line where the goal area merges with it).

When the kick-off is taken or when a resumption of play takes place after a goal has been scored, both linesmen must stand at midfield.

After the Game

The linesman closer to the dressrooms is usually required to stay by them in order to better observe the exit of the players from the field; by doing so they can spot any possible misconduct which may occur and report it to the referee. Whenever the situation and conditions are such as to constitute a potential danger to the safety of the referee, it is the duty of the linesmen to remain very close to the referee until he has been able to leave the playground safely. In any case, the linesmen are required, whenever necessary, to support the actions and the prestige of the referee.

Brief Summary of Duties and Responsibilities of Linesmen

Chapter 26

It must be emphasized quite clearly that whatever has been outlined in chapters 3, 4, 5, and 6, Part Three is a thorough outline of fundamental duties and responsibilities incumbent upon the referee and the linesmen, only if neutral. A brief summary and a few clarifying points to be remembered follow:

1. the diagonal system of control should be followed by the three officials at all times (see Diagram 2 on p. 150);

2. all standard set of signals should be briefly reviewed before the game by both the officials; the referee shall then indicate which particular signals should be used in given situations;

3. the linesman should signal an infraction by immediately raising the flag, vertically at first and then moving it slightly to the right and to the left (waving), but only once, and make sure that the referee's attention has been attracted;

4. the linesman should immediately stop running when signaling any infraction, stand rigid and straight, and face the field of play;

5. the linesman should indicate, after gaining the referee's attention, which way the free-kick or throw-in should be taken to restart the game. The arm and flag should be at a 45-degree angle and held rigid;

6. the linesman should signal off-side by keeping the arm and the flag vertical, while the free arm should indicate which player was off-side;

7. in the case of other infractions, the linesman who is holding the flag raised (at a 45-degree angle) should indicate with the free arm, or body movements, what type of infraction is being called. Having completed that particular signal, he should use the international signal one-arm-

vertical to indicate an indirect free-kick if that applies. Lack of this indirect signal in addition to the type of infraction indicated will automatically tell the referee that a direct free-kick should be awarded, if and when that situation applies;

8. having signaled off-side and having the referee stopped the game, the linesman should stay exactly in line with the position from which the free-kick is to be taken, so as to indicate this position to players and the referee as well until the game is correctly restarted;

9. when infractions are committed inside the penalty area by defenders which are considered by the linesmen to be penalty decisions, the linesman must refrain from pointing toward the penalty spot. This may create embarrassment for the referee if he does not agree and intends to refuse any penalty appeal. Instead the linesman should observe the referee verify his position, then decide if the referee could have clearly seen the incident. It is then up to the linesman to quickly assess the situation and judge that it is his duty, and a very necessary one, to inform the referee that a penalty offense has occurred. Only he can assess this most vital decision, to call or not to call, if the referee did or did not see it clearly.

10. the linesman should not indicate direction, but first raise his flag vertically, then indicate the offense, and finally move to a position on the side-line near the corner flag and wait until the penalty call is actually affirmed by the referee before moving into the correct position for the actual penalty kick;

11. the linesman should not signal that a goal has been scored unless a situation has arisen whereby the decision must be absolutely his. For example, when the ball strikes the underside of the cross-bar, bounces down fully behind the goal-line, and spins back into play. In this or similar situations, based upon his own location and viewpoint at the time, the referee will indicate to the linesman that a decision by him is needed. The linesman must then raise his flag to signal a goal and point toward the center of the field. With the above or similar exceptions, a linesman should not raise his flag when he considers that a legitimate goal has been scored. He should first check that the referee is awarding or preparing to award the goal subject to his (the linesman's) confirmation. The linesman should then run smartly toward the half-way line into a restart game position. Should the linesman feel that a goal should not be allowed for some valid reason the referee may not be aware of, the linesman should not raise his flag, but, instead, stand rigidly at attention at the point where he was when the goal was scored, and until such time the referee either confers with him or indicates that a final, irrevocable decision has been made and that he, the linesman, must at once end his "no goal" indication and

assume his position for the game's restart. Linesmen must accept the notion that the decision to confer rests entirely with the referee and they should accept without question any overruling signal from him in the interest of the overall game control and in the spirit of total cooperation. The only further exception to the linesman's duties not to signal a goal is in the event that a signal (for example, an off-side) was already in effect when the goal was scored. In this case, a linesman should maintain that effective signal until it is accepted or rejected. All signals should be maintained for a reasonable but short period to give fellow officials time to observe them. However, if the referee fails to see a linesman's signal and play is proceeding to a more serious situation, then the linesman should end his current signal, resume his duties, and revert to the rigid stance position if a goal then immediately results, albeit unfairly, due to the prior infringement being missed;

12. linesmen must check that the ball is always positioned correctly, that the corner flag is correctly placed (i.e., properly nailed to the ground), and that no defender is encroaching at corners which are taken on his side of the goal. All the above observations must be made before taking up a final position;

13. linesmen's duties are to assist the referee. They must signal when the whole of the ball passes over the goal-line or the side-lines, and to indicate also which side is entitled to the goal-kick or throw-in;

14. linesmen are usually in the best position to observe which side is entitled to the throw-in, but if the play is in the referee's diagonal, he can often observe the position better than the linesman who is upfield at the half-way line. Referees should accept the throw-in decision under these circumstances, and the linesmen should observe if the referee is making the decision in the opposite half to that in which he is operating himself. If so, he should refrain from signaling and thereby avoid a confusion of signals if their two opinions differ. This is truly cooperation;

15. at the end of each period, linesmen should indicate time remaining to the referee during the last five minutes of play. This indication should be given with the number of fingers equivalent to the minutes remaining. The signal is given by extending fingers of the free hand down by the outside of the thigh for five to one minute. Full time is indicated by placing the free arm firmly across the chest. The referee, having once received a time signal, should immediately check it by reference to the other linesman and his own watch, and have no need to reverify thereafter. The time given shall be that shown on the regular watch and make no allowance for time- outs. Time allowance should be strictly the responsibility of the referee based on his stop watch and

he shall recognize that time indicated by the linesmen is minus all delays (any of them at least sixty seconds in duration);

16. linesmen should indicate verbal abuse from players by pointing to the player concerned with the free hand and then tapping the index finger on their own bottom lip;

17. linesmen should also be aware of players entering or leaving the field of play without the referee's permission, trainers or others encroaching on the field, officials coaching during the play, or any other off-field irregularities;

18. linesmen should assist referees by themselves dealing with irregularities if possible rather than interrupt a game or the referee unduly;

19. all three officials should note the goals, the time the goals were scored, the scorer as well as the offense, and the offender when cautions or ejections are issued. Some competitions do not require linesmen to report these incidents, but may later ask a linesman for verification in a disputed case. In anticipation of the latter, linesmen should keep a record of significant episodes or incidents which may occur during a game;

20. two officials should never be doing one job if cooperating fully. For example, at free kicks near goals by attackers, the referee can adequately judge off-side. Therefore it is normal and recommended that the linesman take position at the goal line in the event of a shot on goal directly from the free-kick;

21. linesmen should cut across the corner of the field, if play allows it, following a corner-kick or a defensively cleared penalty-kick in order to regain off-side and side-line positions as quickly as possible. If able to delay his movements, the referee will assist the linesman by covering the off-side personally as long as he can safely do so;

22. when independent time clocks are used, even though they are unofficial, the linesmen should check to see that the clock is operated simultaneously with the referee's time-out and time-in signals;

23. linesmen should be instructed to keep up with the second rearmost player. This includes, of course, the goalkeeper. It does not mean the second rearmost defender but the player who is second from the goal line and that may be a forward or a defender. Linesmen are primarily responsible for off-side decisions and should always be appropriately positioned in order to give an absolute decision. The only exceptions to this would be when linesmen are repositioned by the referee for free-kicks near goal or are returning from corner-kick type situations, at which time coverage of the off-side will be retained by the referee;

24. all three officials should have jointly inspected the field and appurtenances thereon upon their arrival, but linesmen should again physically

check their respective half of the field before the kick-off and visually scan the field prior to resumption of the game after the half-time interval;

25. linesmen should always appear to be fully alert from the time they enter the field to the time they leave;

26. linesmen should always be aware to keep the flag unfurled and signal clearly;

27. linesmen should always follow every long ball right to the goal line or the goalkeeper no matter how futile this may appear;

28. linesmen should never show to be disturbed when overruled by the referee. They must remember that if theirs or the referee's opinions differ, both, however, feel correct, but one is obviously wrong and that one is certainly not the referee;

29. linesmen should never change hands with the flag to signal opposite directions. There may come a day when they will accidentally drop the flag. Downfield signals can be made easily with the arm across the body and a slight twist from the waist;

30. linesmen shall never discuss any subject with bench personnel unless their duties absolutely require it;

31. linesmen must not signal off-side if the player concerned is obviously too far out of the immediate play to be interfering either with it or his opponents;

32. linesmen must not signal off-side or infractions immediately if a distinct advantage may be arising to the offended team. The delay should be, obviously, momentary, but it is important to remember the old saying, "Better a decision that is late and right than one too early and possibly wrong."

33. linesmen should remember the golden rule which best assists their cooperation and the referee:
    a. If they don't raise their flag, do they fail the referee?
    b. If they raise their flag, do they embarrass him?

The application of the aforementioned golden rule depends largely on the discretionary ability (and intelligence) of the linesmen, and on that discretionary ability rests their real ability as linesmen.

Summary of Duties and Responsibilities of Referees

Chapter 27

1. To enforce the laws of the game and decide any disputed point.
2. To keep detailed and accurate record of entire game: kick- off, time goals scored, details of misconducts, etc.
3. To stop the game for an infringements of the laws of the game, for interference from spectators, or for any other cause he deems necessary.
4. To caution any player guilty of misconduct or ungentlemanly behavior and suspend said player from further participation if he persists.
5. To allow no person other than the players and the linesmen to enter the field of play without his express permission.
6. To stop the game if, in his opinion, a player is seriously injured and to have him removed as quickly as possible in order to immediately resume the game. If a player is only slightly injured, the game shall not be stopped until the ball has ceased to be in play. A player who is able to go to the touch line or goal line for attention shall not be treated on the field of play.
7. To suspend from further participation in the game, without previous caution, any player guilty of violent conduct.
8. To signal and recommence correctly after all stoppages.
9. To see that the ball meets with all the requirements set forth in Law 2.
10. To see that offenders do not gain unfairly by any misconduct.
11. To refrain from penalizing where, by doing so, he would give an advantage to the offending side ("Advantage Clause").

12. To remember that he is all powerful, knows and understands all seventeen laws thoroughly and is well aware of that power.

13. That there is nothing that any player, coach, manager, spectator, or any outside agency can do to interfere with the game which cannot be officially dealt with by the referee within the framework of the laws of the game. Every single possible infraction or incident is referred to and covered by the laws of the game.

14. To use all his powers in a judicious manner.

15. To display a common sense attitude (referees call it Law 18).

16. To intelligently use discretion.

17. To display good personality, pleasant manner, sense of humor, and understanding.

18. To show ability to adopt a firm, positive and immediate attitude with serious offenders in a manner which is unmistaken.

19. All aforementioned abilities form the basic qualities of a good official.

20. Never to show his powers in a dictatorial and bombastic attitude, or with little respect or understanding of the players, if he wishes to effectively control the game. He will rarely gain the respect of players, coaches and spectators with such attitude. He may become a good referee, but never a great referee.

21. To do his best (duty) to gain the respect of all who take part in the game.

22. To make sure that the game is played in a sporting manner.

23. To ensure that the game is a thoroughly enjoyable event rather than merely a contest.

24. To ensure above all that all players end the game perfectly happy in spirit and sound in limb.

25. To watch for hand faults at throw-ins while linesmen shall indicate foot faults by raising the flag and raising a foot slightly or stepping into the field to indicate the type of foot-fault concerned.

26. To make sure that ejected players go directly to the dressing room and take no further part in the game.

27. To keep in mind significant duties toward: spectators, the league, the participating clubs, the players, the whole game of soccer, the other officials, and themselves.

A. Spectators:

Should have adequate viewing and be safely located. Foggy conditions, poor floodlighting, heavy snow or ice make viewing and accommodations very difficult. The referee has the sole responsibility to declare the facilities and the playing field as well inadequate. He must see that the game is played with as little delay as possible. Occasionally even though not required to do so, there is no loss of dignity involved if an official can retrieve a ball more quickly and easier than a ball boy or a player. Be insistent on quick restarts after all stoppages and firm with all offenders. Keep the game flowing by not calling very minor infractions which have no serious impact on the game, unless blatant or repetitious. Apply the advantage clause whenever it is safely possible. See that team colors don't clash and that all players can be distinguished easily.

B. *The League:*

As a league official, the referee represents the highest official (president, executive official, or commissioner) for the period surrounding his duties before, during and after the game. He should uphold all regulations which affect and apply to referees. He should perform his duties with the highest integrity and honesty, make all decisions according to the laws, firmly, and judiciously. Accept all his appointments, and arrive in good time at the game. To be aware of being a professional, employed as a top class official with a thorough knowledge of the laws of the game, to remain that way, and also keep in good physical condition. To report irregularities, including misconduct by players or others which would reflect badly upon the league (or association). The report (see Appendix 4) filed quickly, should be clear and factual. Never to ridicule the league, or association, its members, players, or fellow officials.

C. *Participating Clubs:*

Once they have made a decision to play the game they should make every effort to see that it is played through if possible. When disputes between the clubs occur, every effort should be made to settle them without bias to either club. The referee should be diplomatic first and resort to strict compliance with the laws and regulations when diplomacy seems inadequate to resolve the dispute. The referee should inform, whenever possible, the home club if he should need accommodations. He should call the club immediately upon arrival in the city to indicate his location in the event of emergency. He should contact both managers immediately upon his arrival at the stadium (or playing location) to familiarize himself with local arrangements for the game or special instructions which the league may have issued the referee via the clubs. To discuss substitution procedures with the coaches and all other items stipulated with pre-game procedures (discussed later). To consider his responsibilities to opponents and to all concerned when requested to allow special items, such as longer than normal half-time shows or similar events, and then, if possible, cooperate within reasonable limitations.

D. The Players:

Make sure that all unscrupulous players are strictly kept in check. This can be achieved by adopting a very positive and firm attitude immediately after the game commences. It is a proven fact that some players who are ejected arrive in that situation through earlier relaxation on the part of the referee. Ejections often arise from retaliations when a player feels that the opponent has been dealt with too leniently or not at all in some previous incident, and this reflects upon the referee. Obviously violence or serious fouls occur impulsively and without previous warning on some occasions. Also, more significantly, a player may have a preconditioned attitude to the game which causes him to commit serious actions early in the game. Even this type of player may be saved by positive, sound, well chosen words of advice firmly presented at the time of an offense. To be mindful that the primary duty is to control the game and protect the participants. To remember that the need to protect players far outweighs all other considerations, and if the ejection of a player is necessary to achieve this, then in the interest of all others, the ejection must be made. To extend the player the same amount of respect which you expect from him toward you as a referee. To treat him, the player, in a friendly manner with a manly attitude. Do not belittle a player by ridiculing either his play or personality. If, on the other hand, a player attempts to ridicule an official, then without returning that ridicule, the law provides positive ways to deal with dissent or ungentlemanly conduct, and this discipline must be applied rigidly. Do not restrict players who play the game hard (aggressively) or seek to gain the ball by sheer determination rather than skill. It is easy to mistake hard play for foul play. Many injuries are avoided rather than caused when two players go firmly into a tackle rather than holding back. But what was really a good hefty fair charge, albeit hard, can look like a violent one if the opponent draws back or is unbalanced at the moment of contact, or if you, the referee, have an angled view of the incident. Always make an effort to gain the confidence of players by words of advice at minor infractions rather than using aggressive warnings. To remember that if the offense is fairly harsh or a repetition (of a previous similar one), warn the player in a firm, positive manner than that as a dictator. If the offense is particularly bad (violent) deal with it in the same quick manner with hard words, severe warning or caution or ejection according to the offense. Adopt an attitude which indicates your control of that particular situation and gain the confidence of all other players who feel the need for protection, yet positively warn any other would-be offender. Explanation of decisions, always brief and concise, never time-wasting, often helps to control situations. To call out the offense and penalty, for instance . . . "Pushing, #3 of Reds a direct kick," will often resist further objections and avoid being involved in any form of arguments. Often a good, conscientious captain can be of assistance when resolving difficult situations and until you meet the very occasional player who is negative in this regard, then presume that a captain will respond when asked to assist. A good referee will rarely have to seek such assistance in any case. Remember many players with a reputation for robust play or violent manner will often surprise you, the referee, with their responsive attitude when handled in a positive and, why not, fatherly, persuasive manner. This can very often resolve what may otherwise turn out to be a very serious incident later if the aggression is met with polite aggressiveness by the referee.

E. The game of soccer:

a. Long delays at throw-ins.

b. Players who deliberately walk down the line several yards when taking a throw-in, knowing that the referee will have to recall them and legally waste time.

c. Players deliberately encroaching at free-kicks or corner-kicks.

d. Delays by the kicker at taking the free-kick.

e. Goalkeepers or other defenders who walk to the ball, inspect it or move it after it has already been placed for a penalty-kick.

f. Defenders who fail to stand ten yards away from free-kicks (rear goals).

g. Corner kickers who take out the flag knowing that it will have to be replaced prior to the kick.

h. Players who fake injuries or sit down requesting attention, when only very slightly disabled. Be firm with this action but careful; very few referees have medical knowledge so, if in doubt, have the player receive attention. Nevertheless fake injuries are usually very definitively faked, therefore they must be dealt with sternly.

i. Don't allow too many outsiders on the field. Call the official team trainers alone for injuries and, if requested by him, allow the club doctor to be called later. Remove both the trainer and the doctor as soon as possible. Remove seriously injured players as soon as it is safe to do so and restart as quickly as possible.

j. Effect substitution changes quickly. Be alert to possible delays on substitutions which are deliberate and intended to take out the momentum of the opponents who are temporarily in command of the game.

k. See that the ejected players, injured players, or substitutes leave the field by the nearest way and do not walk long distances on the playing area.

l. Don't engage in lengthy discussions over infractions and get the game moving quickly: both temper and mood of the game will return to normal much quicker.

m. Discourage all players from delaying tactics, and if it is ever necessary to warn or caution for the offense, use the occasion in a manner that will indicate your feelings to every other player. Also inform the team captain exactly what punishment you are awarding and why.

n. Discourage players who kick the ball out of play after an infraction has been called, or continue to play knowing that the whistle has already blown.

o. See that the game starts at the official time and limit the half-time interval to five minutes inside the dressing room unless extenuating circumstances necessitate other actions.

See that the laws of F.I.F.A. and those of the league are fully and fairly applied. Promote the game by speaking highly of this great, worldwide sport. Publicize it at every opportunity. Volunteer your services to local organizations to promote the game at all levels. As you become highly recognized professionally, you are the highest qualified, best-trained official within the country. Spread that knowledge and your experience to every possible corner with the intention of trying to benefit all other officials, players, coaches or children who you feel can benefit from your advice and experience.

F. The other officials:
It is your duty to have confidence in them. Rely upon their judgment until such time you are faced with unreliable or ineffective assistance which is, encouragingly, become more rare with our continued experience and the improved standards. Don't be too hasty to criticize but, if you do so, be constructive with advice rather than purely critical in a negative fashion and discuss things with the person concerned, not with others. As a referee, use your linesmen, and as a linesman, respect the referee's responsibilities and accept his prerogative powers to overrule you. Pass on your knowledge to fellow referees in your local referee discussion groups and recruit other referees by your example and enthusiasm.

G. To ourselves:
After consideration for every other single factor mentioned above, consider then your duty to yourself. Remember that you have to control the game ultimately. Don't jeopardize your control for any other outside consideration. Don't allow unscrupulous team coaches

or officials to interfere with your job, and take advantage by manipulating, by obtaining illegal substitutions, by influencing your decisions by any direct or indirect pressures. Don't become too familiar with players, remain friendly but firm on the field, and avoid undue social contact off it. Keep physically fit, refresh your memory of the laws constantly. Answer any correspondence quickly. Make game reports within a few hours after the game when any recollection is still vivid. Be efficient, be smart, wear a neat uniform, carry good whistles, watches, and other equipment. Look and act professional. Avoid making possible mistakes. When ejecting a player, be accurate about the number and name of the culprit. Remember, after the game, to check with fellow officials that a caution was made and recorded. As far as identity of players is concerned, there must be complete agreement between the three officials. Finally be reasonable and understanding to the player who effusively enjoys celebrating a goal just scored.

Brief Summary of Most Indirect Free Kicks

Chapter 28

1. When a player rejoins the team without the referee's permission.
2. On a kick-off, the kicker plays the ball again before the same has been played by another player.
3. After a goal is scored directly on a kick-off, a goal kick, and a throw-in, a corner-kick is assessed if a goal is scored directly into own goal by a player kicking the ball on a goal-kick. Also, on a free-kick from outside the penalty area the ball goes into own goal directly, a corner-kick shall also be assessed. If the free kick is taken from inside the penalty area, it must be repeated.
4. The goalkeeper stops the ball with one hand while hanging with the other on the cross-bar.
5. When an off-side is called.
6. When an unfair charge is called.
7. On a penalty-kick, when the kicker plays the ball again after the same has hit the cross-bar or a goal post.
8. On a dangerous play.
9. When the goalkeeper is charged in his own area.
10. When a forward interferes with the goalkeeper who is about to release the ball.
11. When charging the goalkeeper in his own area while in possession of the ball.
12. When a forward standing outside the field protrudes a leg inside the field deviating the ball into goal (no goal, or course).

13. When a player protests a referee's decision causing some disturbance while the play is in progress.

14. When the goalkeeper stops the trajectory of the ball which clearly appears to be heading into goal with any object or stone.

15. When a player calls the ball from an opponent (unfair and deceptive play).

16. When a player uses obscene or abusive language or insults the referee.

17. When a player dissents from a referee's decision and/or strikes him intentionally.

18. When a player insults or strikes an official linesman.

19. On a penalty-kick if a goal has been scored while a forward was standing inside the penalty area.

20. When, on a throw-in, a player plays the ball immediately after throwing it.

21. On a throw-in, when the same player infringes the law a second time.

22. On a throw-in, when the ball is thrown against an opponent violently, not with the clear purpose of having the ball bouncing off an opponent in order to replay it.

23. When a player leans on the shoulders of another player of his own team standing in front of him in order to more easily head the ball.

24. When a player stretches his arms to obstruct an opponent stepping from side to side, moving his arms up and down to delay his opponent's moves even without bodily contact.

25. If a goalkeeper intentionally lies on the ball longer than necessary (makes no apparent attempt to play it quickly).

26. When a player charges an opponent fairly while the ball is not within playing distance.

27. When a player attempts to kick the ball from the opponent goalkeeper's hands.

28. On a goal-kick, if the ball travels in the air, crosses the penalty area (while in the air) but is propelled back by a sudden burst of wind which sends it into goal after being touched by a defensor.

29. On a corner-kick, when the kicker plays the ball again after the same has bounced off the referee or a linesman, but not off another player.

APPENDIX 1

Dimensions of the Playground

The dimensions of the field of play are the fundamental ingredients in the game of soccer. The measurements must be strictly adhered to, as required by the competent authority. The following are the measurements of a playground, as anyone would find in any rules book published in any language. The use of the metric system is highly recommended.

130 yards	120 Meters.
120 "	110 "
110 "	100 "
100 "	90 "
80 "	75 "
70 "	64 "
50 "	45 "
18 "	16.50 "
12 "	11 "
10 "	9.15 "
8 "	7.32 "
6 "	5.50 "
1 "	1 " **
8 feet	2.44 "
5 "	1.50 "
28 inches	0.71 "
27 "	0.68 "
5 "	0.12 " ****

**This measurement, which refers to the corner-area, is usually marked meters 1.50 which corresponds approximately to 2 yards. Most countries use the metric system which should be mandatory in this country, the United States.

****This measurement, which refers to the width of the goal-posts, cross-bar, as well as the markings of the field is normally not less than 10 centimeters nor more than 12 cm.

The field of play should always be readied by the host club according to the rules, and all markings should also be well visible. Furthermore the playing field should be, wherever possible, always grassy and its planimetry should also be strictly observed.

It is important to observe a fact so frequently overlooked in the United States. The dimensions of most playing fields are small, generally marked 100 x 50 yards. Too often visiting foreign teams find such dimensions so ridiculously small that their play and strategy are adversely affected. Therefore it becomes obvious that different measurements of a playing field be adopted not only in relation to the age of players (when they are participating in youth competition), but most importantly to the divisional setup or the category, semi-pro, or pro; which is the case with every country-member of FIFA.

The following dimensions should be seriously considered by all leagues or associations, members of the United States Soccer Association, and preferably adopted.

YOUTH LEAGUE

Division	Age	Dimension of Field
AAA	17-18	45-50 X 90-110 Yards
AA	15-16	45-50 X 90-100 "
A	13-14	45 X 90 "
B	11-12	45 X 90 "
C	9-10	40-45 X 80-90 "

As far as a senior league is concerned, the following measurements should be adopted:

SENIOR LEAGUE (semi-pro)

Division	Dimensions
Divisions A (or 1)	65-75 X 110-120 Yards
" B (or 2)	60-70 X 110-120 "
" C (or 3) Yards	50-55 X 100-110 "
" D (or 4)	50 X 100 "
" E (or 5) Minor League– or Youth League	45 X 90 "

It is a frequent occurrence to see that in taking a corner-kick, players find it difficult to take a run at the ball due to lack of adequate space outside the perimetry of the field. In order to enable the players to take corner-kicks properly and to avoid danger from collision, it is desirable that sufficient space be allowed between the touch-lines and the spectators. A second line should be marked, the same as required in international matches, not less than 1.50 m. (5 feet) outside the boundary lines. The home club is responsible for the proper markings of the playing field. When necessary, and if practicable, the goal-lines and the penalty-area lines should be marked again immediately before the match or during the half-time interval. Light-colored flags should be used at the corners, preferably yellow. A reminder to the home club: all goal-posts and cross-bars should be painted white.

The following criteria should be observed in the marking of the field of play:

    a. the materials used should not be dangerous (i.e., not unslacked lime or creosote);

    b. they must not protrude above the surface;

    c. they should not be placed in ruts or hollows;

    d. they should be easily visible according to the nature of the surface of the ground;

    e. they should have a high degree of stability.

Referees should be insistent that flagposts are not less than 1 meter high.

Organization of Soccer from the Grass Roots to the National Level

As indicated above, soccer can be successful in the United States if it is organized the "international way." Let's see how. There are many leagues in this country which, unfortunately, have not been restructured regionally or nationally by the United States Soccer Association. Many attempts have been made, but to organize a professional league to bring just good soccer is totally unacceptable. The national body (U.S.S.A.) should group all teams at the state level, nationwide, and run a normal tournament. At the end of it, the top teams, at least ten, would be grouped into four regional leagues and continue the same round-robin tournament as before. The top winners of this contest, at least four teams from each region, North, East, South, West, would be part of a professional league. In short, there should result the following:

    a. National League (from the entire country): 16 teams
    b. Regional League (four)—(North, East, South, West):
       18-20 teams each
    c. State Leagues (or Associations), each should have at least the
       following format:
           Division A with at least 16 teams
           Division B with at least 16 teams
           Division C with at least 16 teams

Once the above setup is in place, the following will occur every year:

    1. The winner of the National League championship will be the National Champion Team;
    2. The last four teams at the bottom of the standings at the end of the season will be demoted into the regional league, from which one top team (one for each region) will move up to the national league. From each regional league, four teams will drop down to the lower state leagues, or associations. Basically, there should be a concept, well known universally, of promotions and demotions. To be successful the game should be internationalized. What is going on now is not what goes on anywhere else in the world. The principle of demotion and

124

promotion is the best incentive and motivating principle to make the game of soccer more attractive in this country. Many attempts have been made in this country over the past twenty-five years. The professional leagues have come and gone simply because there is not any attraction to bring people to the stadia. Keep in mind that in this country more than 60 percent of the residents are foreign born. Doesn't that tell you something about the future of soccer? People seem to forget that traditional American sports attract only a fraction of the general public, certainly not those new arrivals from either South America or Europe. Ergo, the National Soccer Association should seriously consider the above suggestions and possibly others which should provide the U.S.S.F. with enough material and produce a plan to implement as soon as possible. Remember, the World Championship is just around the corner, 1994. The essential thing is to get a committee in motion and set the machinery of soccer ready to go.

APPENDIX 2

Club Organization

A *club* should be organized according to by-laws and regulations set forth to govern its membership and all activities. The following format ought to be considered by anyone planning to organize a soccer club:

   a. *Membership:* all the names of those who are members of the Board of Directors should be forwarded to the local league, or association;
   b. *Leadership:* all responsibilities must be well outlined and crystal clear;
   c. *By-Laws and Statutes;*
   d. *The Playground:* its location and efficiency must at all times be known and in top condition;
   e. *Official(s):* assigned to the person of the referee: this provision ought to be mandatory for all clubs, for the referee needs assistance the moment he arrives at the assigned place, particularly if he is unfamiliar with the place or not sufficiently fluent in English;
   f. *The Team:* it must include all registered players;
   g. *Responsibility and Commitment:* to the competent league;
   h. *Affiliation to the League, or Association:* all fees must be forwarded to the competent league well ahead of time, long before the starting season;
   i. *Registration of Players:* No confusion should arise as to the forms to be used when registering member players:
      1. to the youth league.
      2. to the senior league.
   j. *Club Members or Authorized Individuals Admitted to the Field:* they are the club leaders, whenever approved by the referee, and other people such as doctors, photographers, trainers, if approved by the referee.

Appendix 3

Appendix B

Referee's Report

The referee's report is the official documentation of the game and constitutes the referee's dutiful assignment. It is of enormous significance, for it reflects all the aspects, facts, and/or incidents which occurred before, during and after the game. It must, therefore, contain in vivid and clear details all the information necessary so that the competent league, or association, can consider without doubts or uncertainty or without the necessity of further clarifications, the game and final score. Furthermore the report must describe in details the actions of cautioned or ejected players and provide the competent league or association with sufficient evidence necessary to warrant any disciplinary actions which may be taken. Thus all referees must be sensitive to the compelling duty entrusted upon them and prepare the report in absolute serenity, without any bias and prejudice toward anyone, without rushing but solicitously. Referees should avoid wordy expressions but describe the facts exactly as they occurred, omitting nothing nor overemphasizing very irrelevant episodes. They, in particular, should very carefully avoid ignoring anything that actually took place nor make any impulsive statements: to minimize, maximize, or overemphasize a particular episode by excessive use of certain adjectives more to express a personal opinion rather than provide valid details, clearly shows lack of mental composure and provides the competent league or association with insufficient factual evidence which will make any disciplinary action quite impossible to take. A proper and adequate report will make the job easier for any league or association. The preparation of the report must, in general, be uniform for all referees; the same uniformity must be observed in officiating, a not-too-impossible task if everyone has diligently *learned* and *understood* the laws of the game. Even though total uniform officiating is quite hard to expect because of temperamental attitude from one individual to another, uniform filling out of the report is possible if it is done in an atmosphere of calm and serenity when, and only when all the facts can be properly reviewed and detailed conscientiously and objectively. The referee must at all times keep in mind that those who have to judge facts or incidents and who have not seen the game, need all the necessary evidence to recreate in their minds quite exactly what actually happened on the field, so that they can duly and exactly evaluate all the facts and take, whenever necessary, the required disciplinary decisions.

The report (see table) should be divided into several sections, as follows.

a. *location* where the *game will be played*, name of the *playing field*, *date*, what *division* or *group*, *starting time*; all the above should be *printed* in the form which is part of the report. The actual starting time will be added by the referee (a *space* should be provided *next* to the *official starting time*). The referee, upon receiving the assignment (which should accompany the form-report) must immediately notify the competent authority, league, or association if he is unable to absolve his duty on the given date and provide ample and valid reasons for not accepting the assignment;

b. *Score*: the referee must mark down the goals scored, the team that scored them, the time up to the minute when each goal was scored, if and when a penalty-kick was taken and its outcome;

c. *Actual starting time: Duration of the Interval between periods: Time when the game ended: Makeup of lost time*. All the data to the above must accurately reflect how, in reality, everything took place. The starting time must accurately be recorded not only with regard to the first period but also to the second, or any additional period if called for by the nature of the competition; for many objections could be raised in the future with regard to the duration of the game. Thus the referee shall not write down that the game started at 3:00 P.M., which may be the official starting time, but the *actual* starting time, if it was, i.e., at 3:14 P.M. It is important to notice that when a game must be extended beyond the two regular periods, an interval of at least five minutes must be granted to the players.

d. *Players without official pass-cards*: Written statements by the team must be attached to the report. All players must be issued official pass-cards by the competent league long before the playing season begins. A strict compliance with the above will avoid future problems of embarrassment. The complete name of the player(s) without the pass-card(s) must be recorded by the referee. The written statement by the player(s) club signed by the club official, possibly the one assigned to the person of the referee, must be received by the referee and attached to the report. A positive identification of the player(s) must be made to the satisfaction of the referee who, otherwise, may refuse permission to that particular player(s) to take part in the game.

e. *Official Line-Up*: The complete name of each player, in the same order as the line-up submitted by each club, must be recorded on the report prior to the game. The captain of the team must be marked on the report (line-up). Next to each player's full name the number of the pass-card must also be written down. Next to the full name of the player allowed to participate without a pass-card, the referee should write W.P.C. (Without Pass Card). To the report, the referee shall attach any pass-cards of players not returned to the club which the referee has kept, if authorized to do so by the competent league or association either as a result of assault or as requested by the league or association or by a club for further verification of the identity of opposing players. The line-ups, two from each club, will be passed, one copy to the opposing club and the other attached to the report, before the start of the game. The referee must proceed to the checking of the players of each team even though the game may not be played, as long as it has been officially scheduled. If one of the two teams doesn't show up, the referee shall check the identity of the players of the other team before or at the time the game is scheduled to start. In any of the above cases, the full names of the players shall be recorded by the referee on the report and forwarded to the competent league or association;

f. *Safety Precautions by the Home Club*: By that expression it is meant not only those entrusted to the police but also those taken by the home club, such as the posting in many areas of the playground in a conspicuous manner, posters which are intended to warn spectators to refrain from ill-advised or violent acts which would negatively reflect the sportsmanship of the spectators and jeopardize future activities by the club if deplorable or violent acts are committed. Such policy, if adopted in the United States nationwide, would be very desirable. The posting of such notices indicates to the competent league or association the concern of the home club and shows its sincere determination to see that a game will be normally played. As far as the number of the police detail present on the field, the referee shall indicate an approximate number in his report. The disciplinary board will determine the adequacy of all safety precautions taken by the home club;

g. *Spectators Behavior*: There are referees who think that the fence separating the public from the playground actually sets a limit on their overall game control. This is wrong. When requested to describe the spectators' behavior—normal, noisy, good, or excellent—the referee is actually extending, as duly required, his judgment beyond the playing field and indicates only the reaction of the spectators to a player's actions or a referee's decision. But when certain specific expressions are used, i.e., ungentlemanly, offensive, threatening, etc., to describe the spectators' behavior, they are quite inadequate to describe the intemperate rowdiness of the spectators which may have affected, even minimally, the outcome of the game, and even after the game, when there have been incidents against players, club officials and/or game officials. When incidents occur during the game, the referee shall record the exact time when they started and the possible reasons, if he is aware of which provoked them. With regard to incidents arising as a result of spectators' behavior before or immediately following the game on the field of play or outside, there are no justifiable excuses unless they have been provoked by a visiting player. In view of such an eventuality, the referee's overall alertness is required, for his vigilant and careful control of the game may provide some significant hints as to the actual cause and effect of the incident;

h. *Behavior of Club Officials*: Club officials are to be regarded as direct collaborators of the league or association. Consequently they must perform, on every occasion and when it is needed, in a manner suitable to their position or responsibility. On any playgrounds the league or association has in the person of the referee its official representative who, in the performance of his duties has, therefore, the right to demand active and factual cooperation by the club officials or their charges. While it is understandable that club officials cannot avoid sudden bursts of violence by the spectators, they can nonetheless do their best to actively contain any violent form of demonstration or prevent minor outbursts, particularly if they occur by degrees, sporadically. The referee's sharp awareness of what takes place can be truly valuable. In such circumstances the referee provides the best example of a valid and effective watchdog for the disciplinary board. When trying to identify individuals who passively and indifferently or even by their despicable example, instead of actively interceding to cool down tempers actually incite the troublemakers to cause more serious incidents, the referee shows his best self. Moreover he shows commendable courage in reporting to the competent league or association (disciplinary board) any club official who has been seen acting irresponsibly, uncooperatively, and has furthermore shown open hostility toward the referee.

Referees are urged to report particularly the names of officials assigned to them, as is customary in most countries outside the United States, prior positive identification which must be made and ascertained. In the case of incidents anywhere on the playground the referee shall report to the competent disciplinary board about the behavior of club officials and players of both teams, how the club officials behaved and what they did in order to normalize the situation, and finally the names of those club officials who either acted effectively to bring about the calm or those who were indifferent or even contributed to deteriorate the situation already tense;

i. *Players' Behavior:* This has to do with the overall behavior of all players, their dedication and discipline which they display before, during, and after the game, toward everyone and above all toward the referee. Including the end of the game, the applicability of the laws of the same case, the disciplinary rules as set forth by the league or association, remain in force and applicable at any time. In order to appropriately and impartially judge the facts and take the necessary actions, the competent league or association needs, not only from the referee and from the linesmen, but also from the game official if there was one, all the evidence pertinent to the facts.

It must also be pointed out, although some might disagree, that the degree of hustle shown by some players or even by an entire team has a very relevant significance in the performance on the field. Such behavior is utterly unsportsmanlike and should be penalized, whether it is a player involved or an entire team. The disciplinary board must be informed; a stiff disciplinary action can be the most effective deterrent against future similar actions which tend to destroy the sport. Only by assessing severe penalties can the true sense of sportsmanship be protected. Luckily, such deplorable negative displays of sportsmanship are very rare;

j. *Players Ejected and Reasons:* The first and utmost step to take is obviously the correct identification of the culprit, right on the field, and to report his full and precise name. No errors of identification are permissible, for the referee possesses all the necessary tools to avoid committing a mistake. The ejection must be justified by serious infraction of the rules of the game. In the case of "striking an opponent," usually the most common, the referee must report the infraction in detail, i.e., by kicking or by the use of fists; the exact minute the incident occurred and, moreover, whether the play was dead or not at the time the alleged fact occurred. The referee should also indicate in his report if the fact occurred as a reaction to some irregular play by an opponent so that the disciplinary board can grant the attenuating circumstance clause, provided the referee mentions in his report the nature of the irregular play which motivated the incident. Furthermore the referee must report if the act was committed in the hope the referee's attention couldn't be attracted; also how the culprit reacted to the referee's decision; whether he left the field without causing unnecessary delay. Failure to abide by the aforesaid, the culprit could be liable of more serious disciplinary sanctions.

Whenever the act is directed against the referee—insults or the like—he shall report exactly the words used by the culprit even if they are obscene. The referee will do a disservice to himself and to the game if he generalizes by reporting such acts under libels such as "abusive or rude language" or "lack of respect, or total disregard for the referee." Such phrases tell little or nothing and provide no evidence to the disciplinary board that can lead to appropriate disciplinary action;

k. *Cautioned Players*: Keeping in mind that caution is a decision taken in the case of mitigated circumstances, all the rules which apply to ejected players are also applicable (with regard to cautioned players). If, for example, a player deliberately strikes an opponent he must be ejected at once. Ejection of players from the game is always final and must never be taken as a precautionary measure. If a referee finds it impossible, because of exceedingly tense atmosphere on the playground, to eject a player guilty of the most serious offense for which ejection is the remedy even with the active cooperation of the captain of the same team, he shall report to the competent disciplinary board all the circumstances related to the episode in the most minute details, specifying also the behavior of the team captain and/or that of the club officials if they were participant in the episode and the extent of it;

l. *Other Incidents*: Under this label are included unfortunate incidents or injuries which should be reported by the referee, particularly when possible injuries occur to players or individuals or to the referee. The referee should, at the end of every game, report the nature, the cause and all the circumstances of the injury in full details, the name of the injured individual as well as the name also of the player who even unintentionally caused the incident. In the case of an injury to a player the referee should report the precise length of time the injured player was away from the field, as well as his general condition after he has re-entered the field of play. If any injuries occur to players prior to the kick-off, the referee should maintain a careful watch, while the game is in progress, on the player(s) who suffered the injury and, if necessary, report it to the competent disciplinary board. The referee shall also report the club which clearly appears responsible for provoking any incidents, and their gravity. It is also extremely important that the referee reports in the most minute and exact details any incidents which may have caused the continuation of the game "pro-forma" with the clear purpose of avoiding much more serious incidents (a possible assault upon the referee). The referee should mark on the report the exact minute when he realized the game had ceased to be played under normal conditions. The referee must also report, at the end of the first and of the second periods, anything a linesman may have pointed out concerning possible incidents undetected by the referee; the linesman's report must be attached to the referee's report;

m. *Advice of Various Nature*: In the case of a team's absence from a game the referee should try to find out the motives, whenever at all possible, informing the competent disciplinary board in enlightening details about the probable reasons of the absence or of the delay (mentioning the length of time). In this regard, the referee should report also the names of players who joined their team late into the game. The referee shall also report if the linesmen have possibly been substituted. Also, temporary suspension of the game or final suspension must be reported in details even though the causes of the suspension originated outside the field of play. In this regard, the referee must at all times keep in mind the minutes that must be made up. All papers attached to the report must be listed on the report itself. The referee shall never pass judgment upon the validity of registration requirements;

n. *Observations (remarks) made on the playground and in the dressrooms*: The referee should report upon the conditions and decorum of the dressrooms, the efficiency and sturdiness of the fence (when required by the competent league or association) around the field of play, and the protective covered tunnel (whenever mandated by the competent association) which connects the dressrooms with the playground; the improper markings on the field of play, etc. The referee should also ascertain that the linesmen are those expressly appointed by the league or association and report their full names. If the linesmen are club-assigned, their identities must be ascertained; if in possession of a pass-card, whenever required by the competent association, the referee should verify its validity and list the number of the pass-card on the line-up. Under no circumstances or for any reason should the referee discuss anything which is, or will be, part of his official report to the disciplinary board, as well as making references in any way to possible disciplinary decisions toward certain players or club officials. The referee should firmly and politely ignore any inquiry as to the above: prudence, he must always remember, is one of the highest qualities he must display. It is advisable to fill out the report by printing, using the typewriter whenever possible in two copies, one of which he will keep in order to refer to it in case of eventual dispute. When filling out the report, the referee should avoid expressing judgment or evaluation upon behavior displayed by club officials, spectators, or players. The incidents must be reported factually and precisely and the responsibilities pointed out. Proper use of simple language is fundamentally required. The report must then be mailed by registered mail if possible or as required by the competent league or association. Whenever a referee is required by the disciplinary board to supply additional details regarding facts which occurred during a game previously officiated, he must abide by the request promptly. In doing so, he must not just simply confirm the contents of his report but clarify all the facts as expressly requested by the disciplinary board.

Appendix 4

Referee's Report—Specimen

Referee's Report

League (or Association):_____

Series:_____ Division:_____

Game Date:_____ Kick-off Time:_____

Played at (field):_____

Between_____ & _____

Score:

    Home Team:_____ Goals:_____

    Away Team:_____ Goals:_____

Actual Kick-off Time:_____

Duration of Interval (Between Periods):_____

Time Game Ended:_____

Made-up Time (minutes):

    First Period:_____

    Second Period:_____

LINE-UP

Club:_____ Club:_____

Player's No.	Player's Name	Pass-card No.	Player's No.	Player's Name	Pass-card No.
1.			1.		
2.			2.		
3.			3.		
4.			4.		
5.			5.		
6.			6.		
7.			7.		
8.			8.		
9.			9.		
10.			10.		
11.			11.		
12.			12.		
13.			13.		
14.			14.		
15.			15.		

Indicate the Captain and the Co-Captain:

_____ / _____

Players without Pass-cards (if any):_____

_____

_____

GOALS SCORED:

      Club_____ at:_____ ', _____ ', _____ ', _____ '
1st half
      Club_____ at:_____ ', _____ ', _____ ', _____ '
      Club_____ at:_____ ', _____ ', _____ ', _____ '
2nd half
      Club_____ at:_____ ', _____ ', _____ ', _____ '

Precautionary Measures Taken by the Club:_____
_____
_____

Players Ejected and Reasons:_____
_____
_____
_____
_____

Players Cautioned:_____
_____
_____
_____
_____

Incidents (on the field or anywhere in the sports complex):_____
_____
_____
_____
_____
_____
_____
_____
_____

Spectators' Behavior:_____
_____
_____

Club Officials' Behavior:_____
_____
_____

Any remarks, on the field or in the dressrooms:_____
_____
_____
_____
_____

Club:_____, _____

Linesmen:

Club:_____, _____

                                            (name)

Referee

_____

Address:_____

                    (street and number)

_____

     (city)   (state)   (zip code)

Enclosures (if any):

_____

_____

_____

Appendix 5

Diagrams

Diagram 1:   The Field of Play

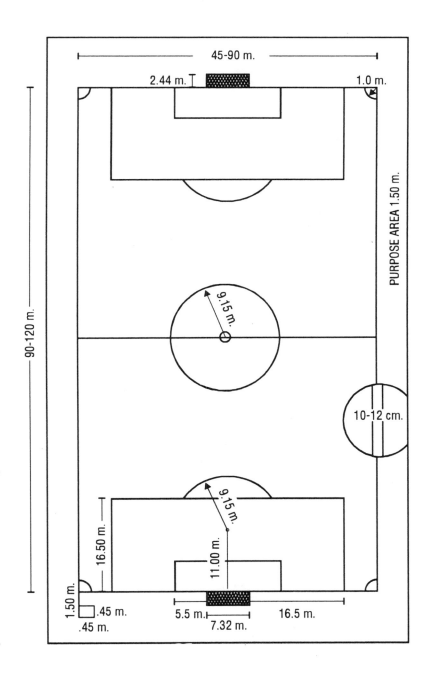

Diagram 2: Diagonal System of Control

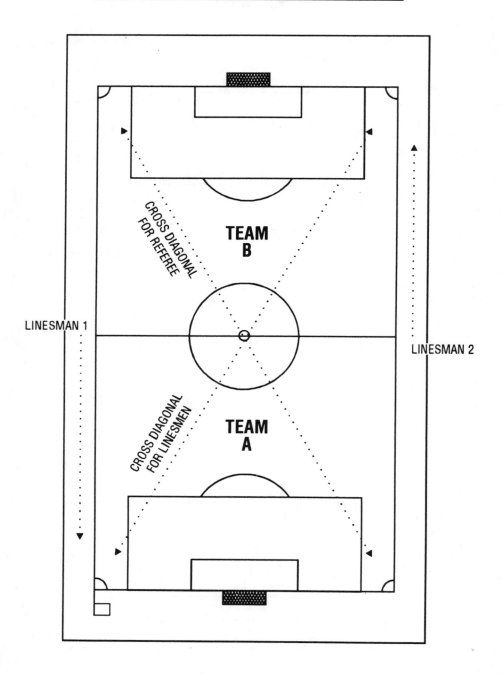

CROSS DIAGONAL FOR REFEREE

TEAM B

CROSS DIAGONAL FOR LINESMEN

TEAM A

LINESMAN 1

LINESMAN 2

Diagram 3:   Start of Game

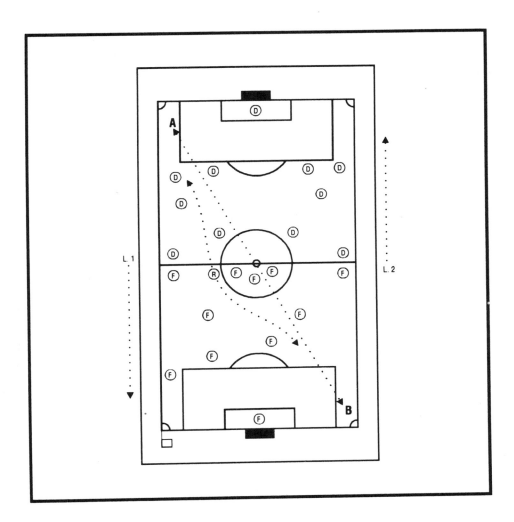

Position of Referee (R) at kick-off. Position of Linesmen (L.1 & L.2). Players' position in midfield (F) & (D). Diagonal A-B followed by Referee according to progress of play.

Diagram 4:   Development of an Attack

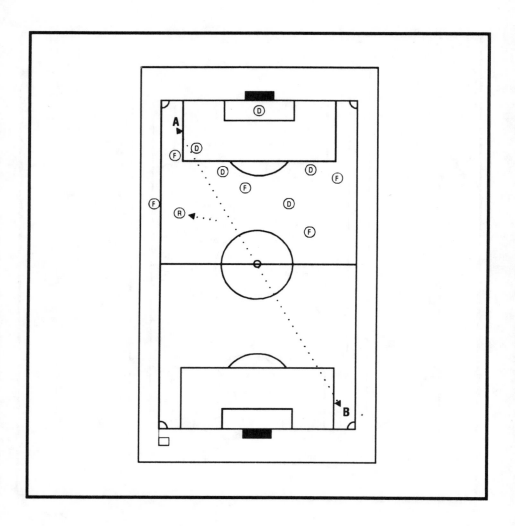

With play developing in team D's own half, Referee (R) moves off diagonal A-B to be closer to play (throw-in by F).

152

Diagram 5:   Corner Kick

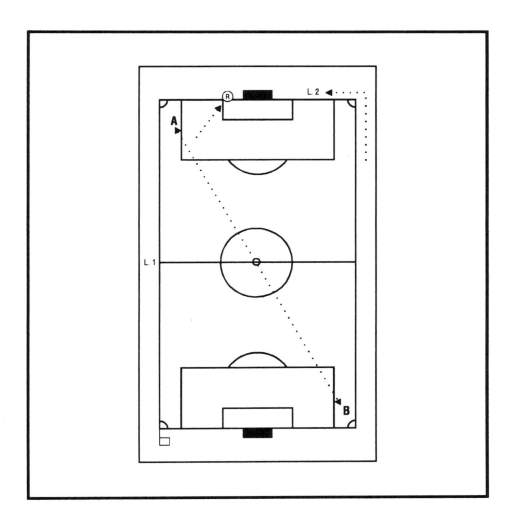

Position of officials (R & L.1, L.2) is standard, no matter at which corner the kick is taken. Position of linesman L.1 is near midfield ready for possible clearance and counter attack, while position of linesman L.2 is closer to junction of penalty area and goal line to observe any incidents or fouls possibly hidden from the referee.

Diagram 6:   The Counter Attack

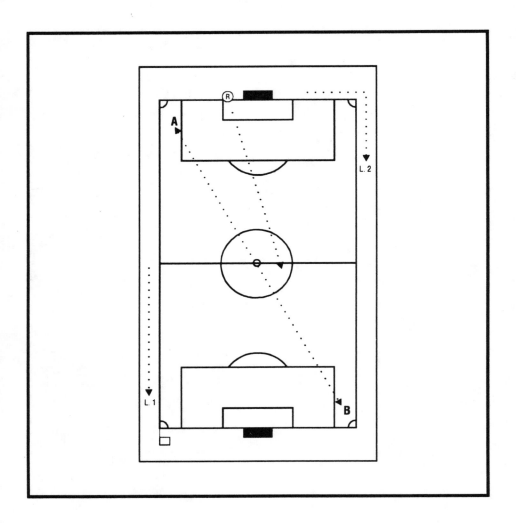

On a breakaway (following a corner kick) referee (R) sprints to regain correct position (along diagonal A-B) following outlined path ——>. A physically fit referee has no difficulty moving very rapidly in the field. Linesman L.1 follows development of play leveling with attack and in position to see any infringements and indicate decisions until referee regains position near play (B). L.2 hurries back to correct position on the side-line.

Diagram 7: The Goal Kick

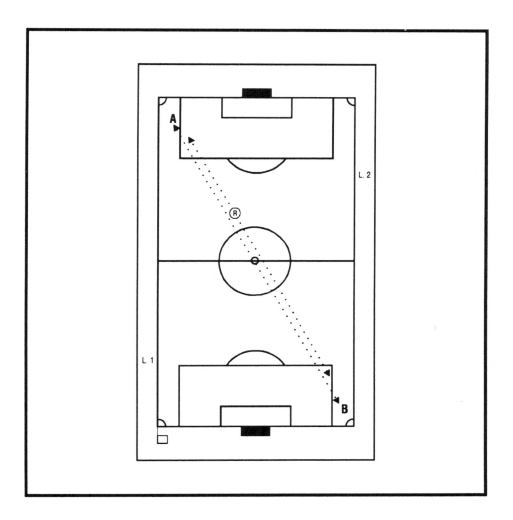

Referee (R) takes position in midfield close to central point of diagonal. Linesman L.1 follows goal kick while linesman L.2 takes position in anticipation of possible attack by Team A taking goal kick.

Diagram 8:   Free-Kick in Midfield

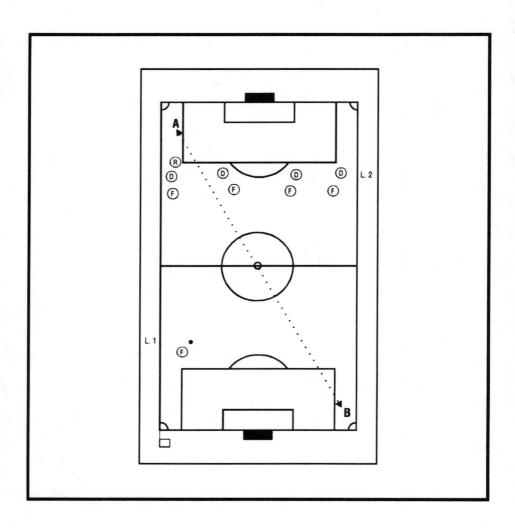

Players D and F line up for free kick. Referee (R) and linesman L.2 level with players and in position to accurately judge any off-side or foul play. Linesman L.1 sees that kick is taken from correct position and also in the right position for a possible counter attack.

Diagram 9:   Free-Kick Near Goal

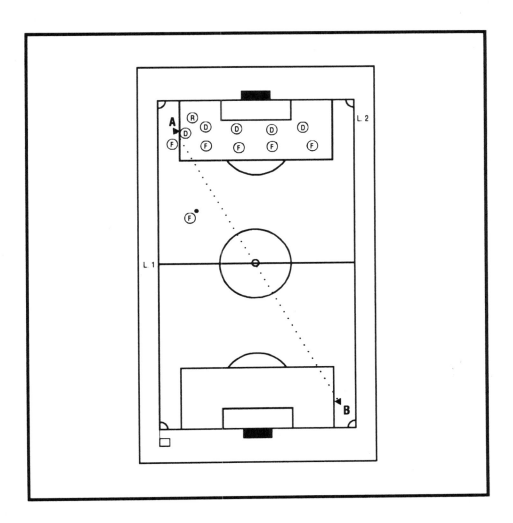

Players D and F line up for free-kick. Referee (R) takes position just off diagonal A-B in order to be able to judge off-side. Linesman L.2 is slightly more advanced but can watch for off-side and fouls and is also in good position to act as goal judge in the even of a direct shot being taken.

Diagram 10: Penalty-Kick

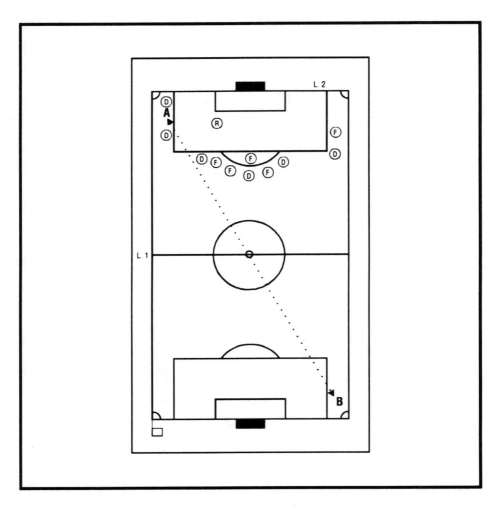

Players D (defensemen) and F (forwards) with the exception of the goalkeeper and the kicker must take position outside the penalty area and at least m. 9.15 (10 yards) from the ball (penalty spot). Goalkeeper is right on goal line, as shown. Referee (R) is in position to see that the kick is properly taken and that no player encroaches inside penalty area. Linesman L.2 watches goalkeeper to see that he does not move illegally and also acts as goal judge. Linesman L.1 is in position should goalkeeper save a goal and start a counter attack.

Diagram 11:   Throw-In

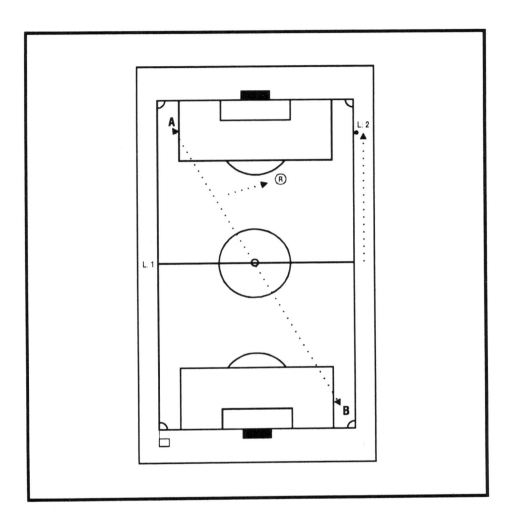

The ball is out of play and Linesman L.2 is in position to indicate position of throw-in and to which side. Referee (R) crosses from diagonal to near center of field to better follow play. Linesman L.1 watches his forward line against possible counter attack.

Diagrams explaining the OFF-SIDE RULE.

The letter F is used to indicate a **forward** (i.e., an attacking player. The letter D is used to indicate a **defensor**.

Diagram 12:   Off-Side

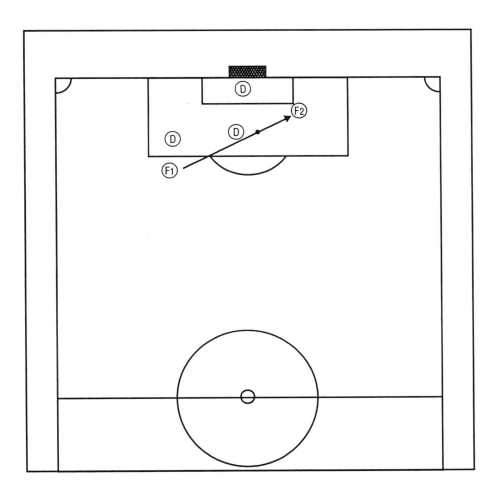

Forward F1 carries the ball and unable to proceed passes it to F2 who is off-side because there is only one opponent (goalkeeper) between him and the goal line.

Diagram 13: Off-Side

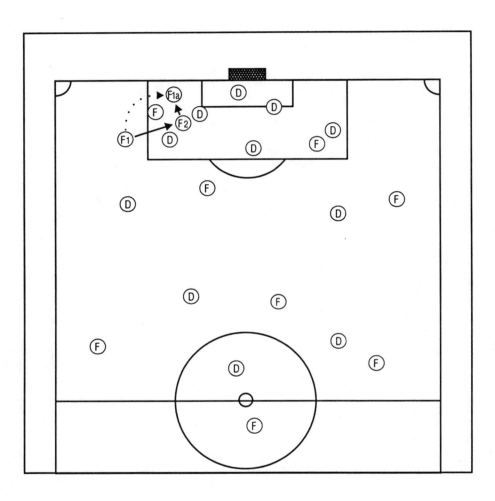

F1 passes the ball to F2 who cannot shoot and passes the ball to F1 (now in position F1a) where he receives the ball from F2. F1 is in offside (position F1a) because he does not have two opponents between himself and the opponents' goal line.*

---

*See the new change regarding the off-side rule.

Diagram 14: Off-Side

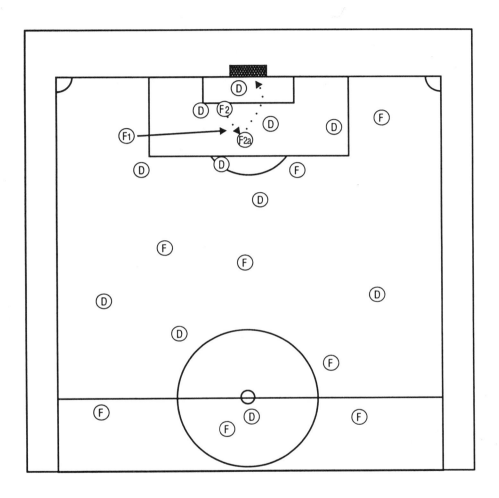

Forward F1 centers the ball. F2 runs to position F2a, then dribbles between two defensemen (D) and scores. F2 was in off-side position and put himself *on-side* (position F2a); no goal.

Diagram 15:   Off-Side

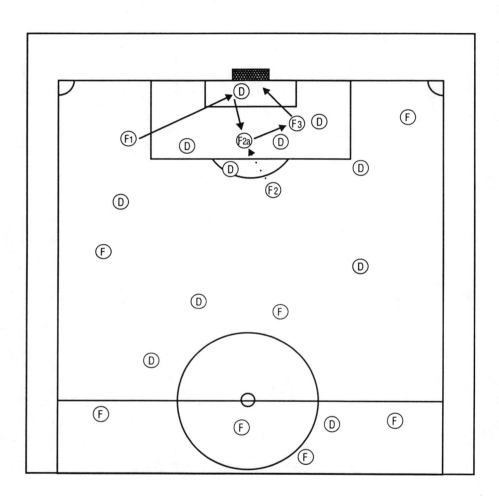

F1 shoots at goal. The ball is played by the goalie and F2 who has in the meantime run to position F2a gets possession of the ball but slips and passes the ball to F3 who scores. F3 is off-side because he is in front of F2 (in position F2a) and when the ball was passed by F2 (position F2a) he did not have two opponents between himself and the opponents' goal line.

Diagram 16:   Off-Side

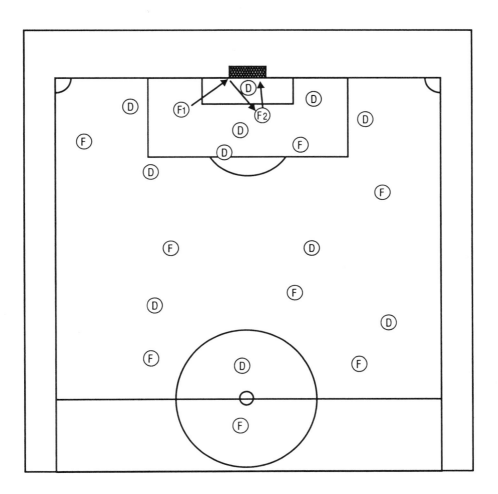

F1 shoots at goal and the ball rebounds from the goal post into play. F2 gets the ball and quickly scores. F2 is off-side because the ball was last played by F1 and he didn't have two opponents between himself and the (opponents') goal line.

Diagram 17: Off-Side

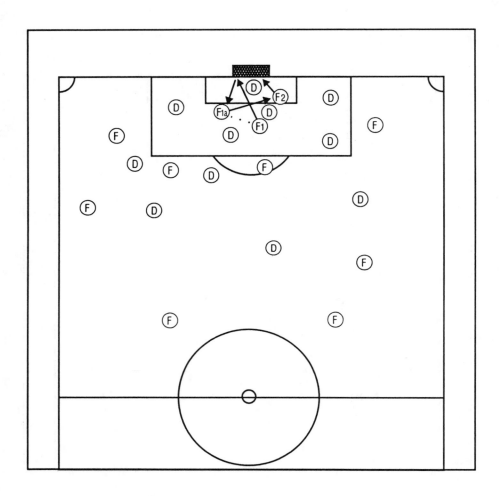

F1 shoots for goal and the ball rebounds from the cross-bar into play. F1 follows up to position F1a where he regains possession of the ball and then passes it to player F2 who has run up on the other side. Player F2 is off-side because the ball was last played by F1, a player on his own side, and when F1 (in position F1a) passed the ball, F2 was in front of the ball and did not have two opponents between himself and the goal line. If F1 had scored directly on the second attempt (position F1a) it would have been a goal.

Diagram 18: Off-Side

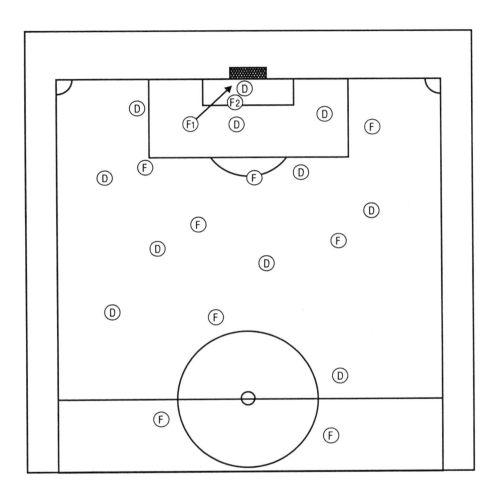

Off-side; obstructing the goalkeeper: F1 shoots for goal and scores. F2, however, obstructs goalie (D) so that he (goalie) cannot get at the ball. The goal must be disallowed because F2 is in an off-side position and although he may not touch the ball himself he cannot, however, interfere in any way with an opponent (the goalie, in the case in point).

Diagram 19:   Off-Side

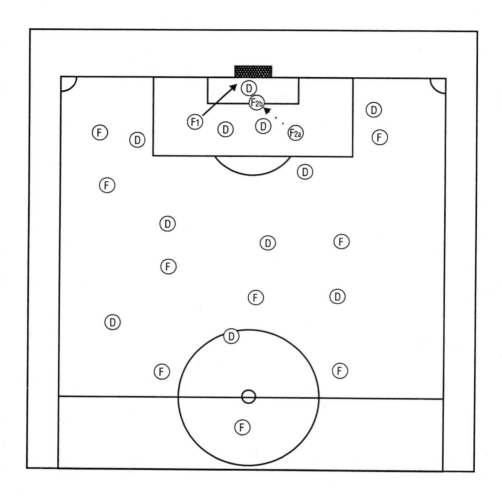

Off-side; obstructing the goalkeeper: F1 shoots for goal. F2 runs from position *a* (F2a) to position *b* (F2b) while the ball is heading toward the goal and prevents the goalie (D) from playing it (the ball) properly. F2b is off-side because he is in front of F1 and does not have two opponents between himself and the goal line when F1 plays the ball. When in this position F2b may not touch the ball himself but he is interfering with an opponent (the goalie).

Diagram 20:   Off-Side

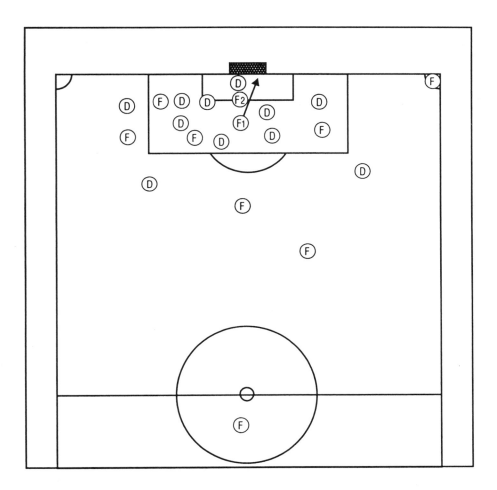

Off-side; obstructing an opponent other than the goalie: F1 shoots for goal. F2 prevents D (goalie) from running in to intercept the ball. F2 is off-side because he is in front of F1 and does not have two opponents between himself and the goal line when F1 plays the ball. F2 cannot, in this position, interfere in any way with an opponent.

Diagram 21:   Off-Side

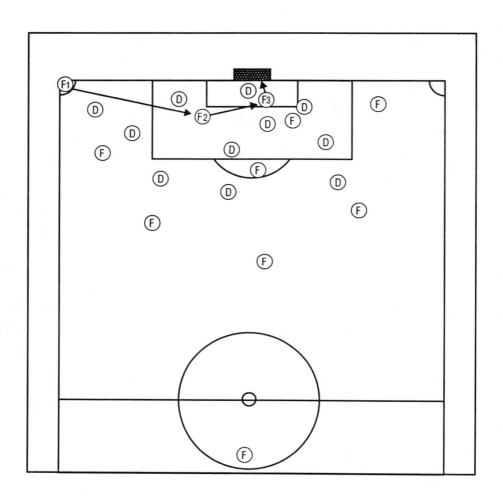

Off-side; after a corner kick: F1 takes a corner kick and the ball goes to
F2. F2 shoot for goal and as the ball is heading toward the goal F3 touches
it. F3 is off-side because after the corner kick has been taken the ball is
last played by F2, a player of his own side, and when F2 played it F3 was
in front of the ball and did not have two opponents between himself and
the goal line.

Diagram 22: Off-Side (Throw-in)

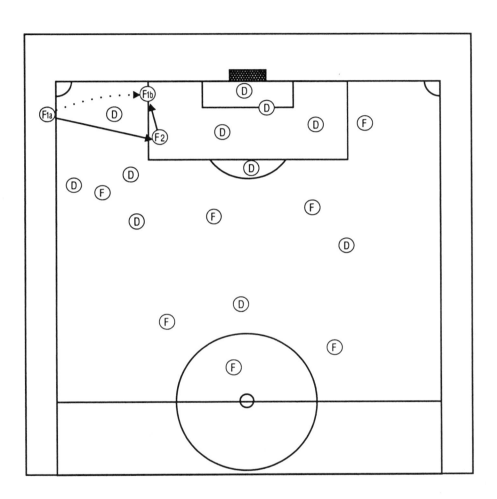

F1 throws to F2 and then runs from the touch line (position F1a) to position F1b. F1b is now offside because he is in front of the ball and has not two opponents between himself and the goal line when the ball was passed forward to him by F2.

Diagram 23: Off-Side

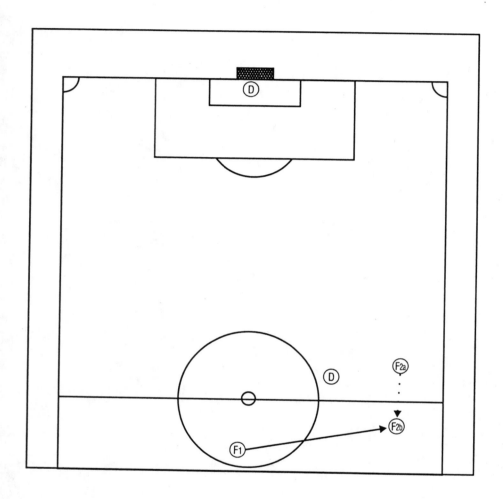

"A player cannot put himself *on side* by running back into his own half of the field of play."

If F2a is in his opponents' half of the field of play and is off side (position) when F1 last played the ball, he cannot put himself *on side* by running back into his own half of the field of play.

Diagram 24:   Off-Side

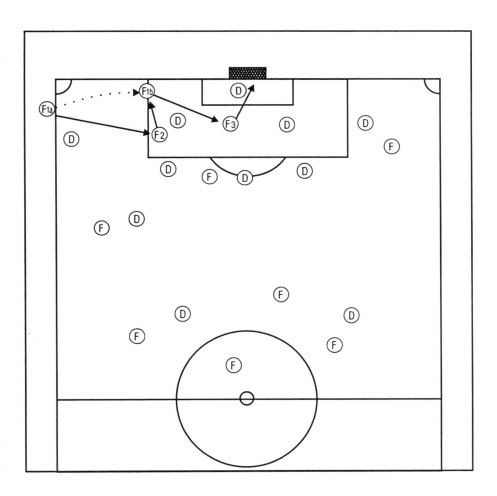

F1a takes a throw-in and throws to F2 who heads the ball forward and F1 gets it in position F1b. From here the ball is passed to F3 who kicks it into goal. *No goal,* for F1b is in an off-side position because he is nearer to his opponents' goal line than the ball when it is played by F2 and does not have two opponents between himself and the goal line. Thus, F1b must be penalized for interfering with play.

Diagram 25: Off-Side

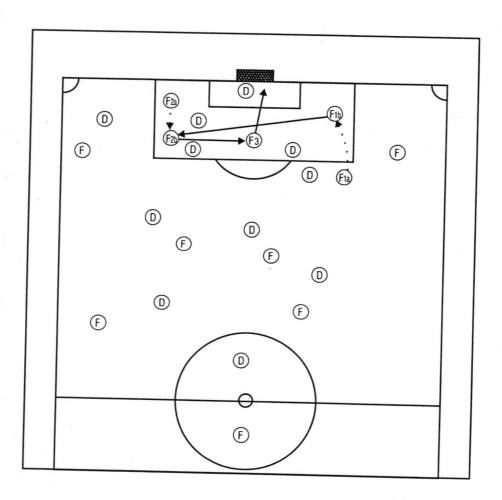

F1a advances with the ball to position F1b from where he centers it. F2a runs to position F2b where he gathers the ball and centers to F3 who kicks it into goal. F2a is off-side (he put himself on-side) when he ran to position F2b after the ball was passed by F1b (or while the ball was being passed by F1b).

Diagram 26:   Off-Side

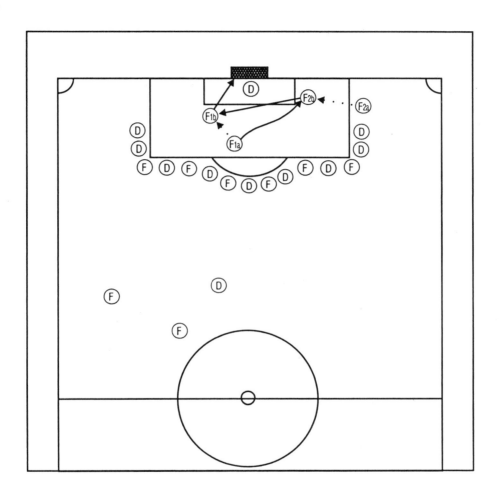

F1a takes a penalty kick. He *slices* the kick and F2a runs into position F2b. From here F2b intercepts the ball and passes it to F1b (new position of F1a). F1b kicks the ball into the goal. F2a is off- side the moment he reaches position F2b where he is nearer to his opponents' goal line and has only one opponent (the goalie) between himself and the opponents' goal line. Therefore, F2b is in an off-side position and must be penalized because, as in this case, he interferes with play.

Diagram 27:   NOT Off-Side

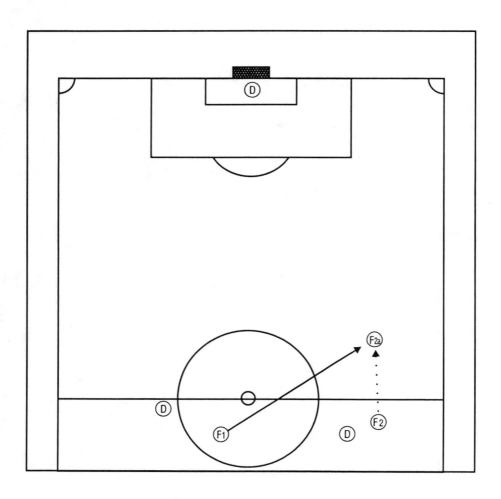

If F2 is on his own half of the field of play he is on-side, although he is in front of the ball and there is only one opponent (the goalie) between himself and the opponents' goal line when F1 last played the ball. F2 is therefore not off-side when he enters his opponents' half of the field of play, provided he does so after the ball has been played by F1.

Diagram 28:   Not Off-Side

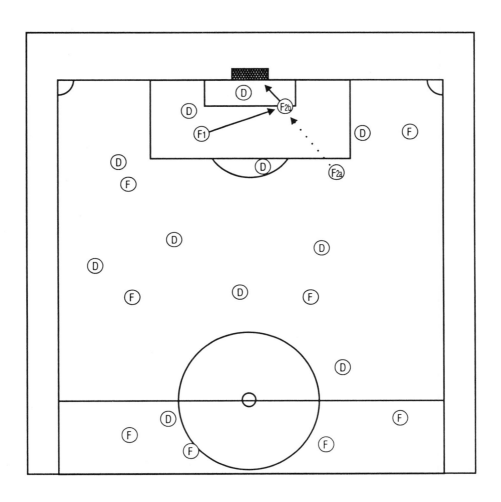

F1 has run the ball up and having an opponent in front passes across the field. F2a runs into position F2b. F2b is not off-side because at the moment the ball was passed by F1 he was not in front of the ball yet and had two opponents between himself and the goal line.

Diagram 29:   Not Off-Side

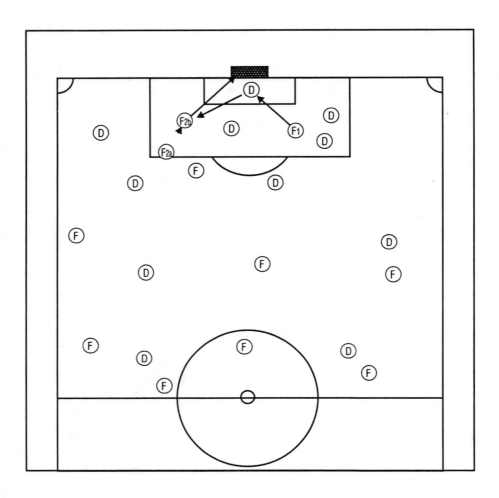

F1 shoots at goal. The ball is played by goalie (D) but F2a who has meanwhile moved to position F2b obtains possession of the ball and scores. F2a, in position F2b although in front of the ball did not have two opponents between himself and the opponents' goal line when the ball was last played by F1, but is not off-side because the ball had been last played by an opponent (the goalie).

Diagram 30: Not Off-Side

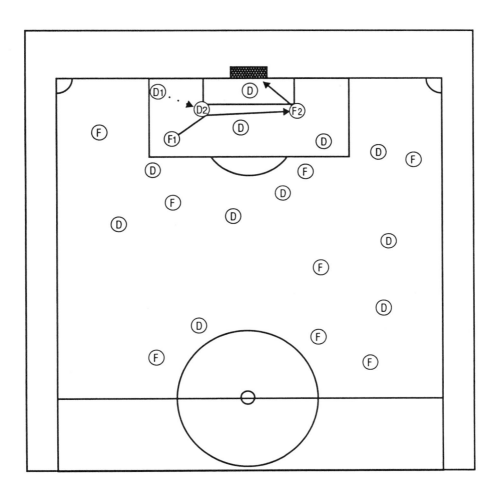

F1 shoots at goal. D1 runs into position D2 to intercept the ball, but it glances off his foot to F2 who scores. F2 is not off-side because although he is in front of the ball and does not have two opponents between himself and the goal line the ball was last played by an opponent (D2).

Diagram 31: Not Off-Side

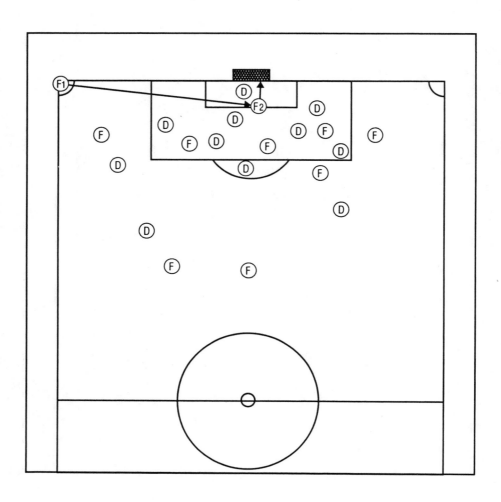

Not off-side; after a corner kick: F1 takes a corner kick and the ball goes to F2 who scores. Although F2 has only one opponent between himself and the goal line he is not off-side because a player cannot be off-side if he gets the ball directly from a corner kick.

Diagram 32:   Not Off-Side

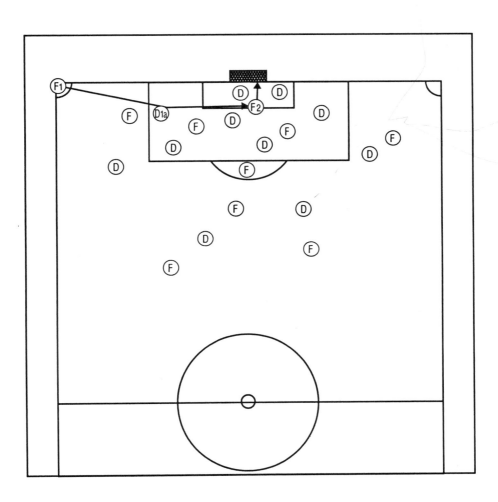

Not off-side; after a corner kick: F1 takes a corner kick and the ball glances off D1a and goes to F2 who scores. F2 is not off-side because the ball was last played by an opponent (D1a).

Diagram 33: Not Off-Side

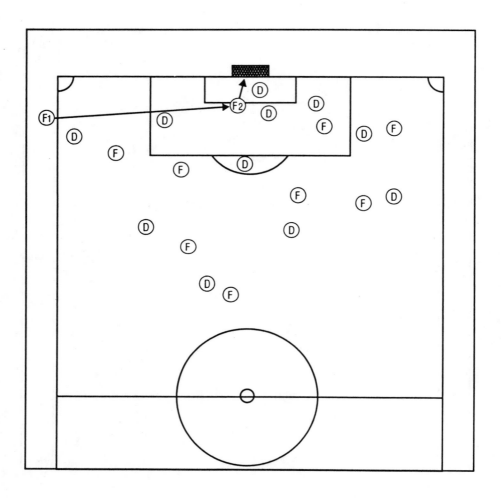

Not off-side; after a throw-in: F1 throws the ball to F2 who scores. Although F2 is in front of the ball and does not have two opponents between himself and the goal line, he is not off-side because a player cannot be off-side from a throw-in.

Diagram 34: Ball In Play or Out Of Play

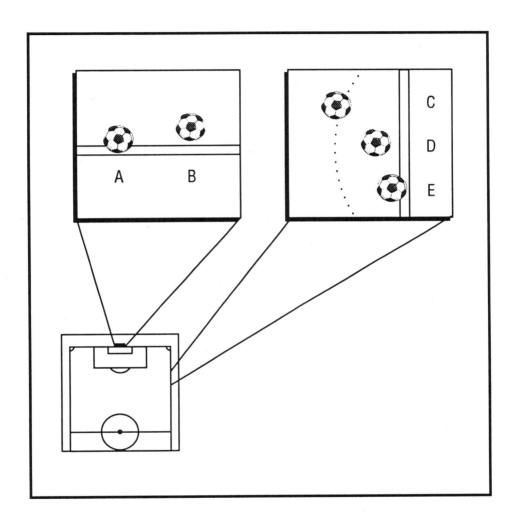

A. Ball still in play (no goal)
B. Ball out of play (goal)
C. Ball still partly on the touch-line
D. Ball entirely out of touch-line (or goal-line)
E. Ball out of play during trajectory

Diagram 35: Throw-In— Position of Player

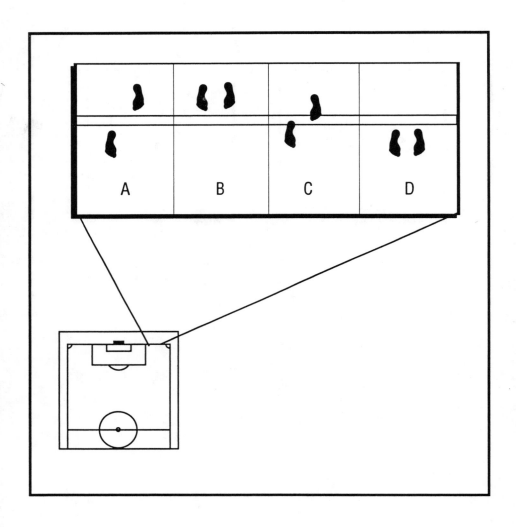

In the diagram above:

Player A: Wrong position at time of throw-in. (Both feet or part thereof *must* at all times be in contact with the ground.)

Player B: Correct position.

Player C: Correct position.

Player D: Wrong position (see A).

The following is to be used by the U.S.S.A. for regional, or state, qualifying rounds (see "Organization of Soccer", p. 124).

TRACKING CHART

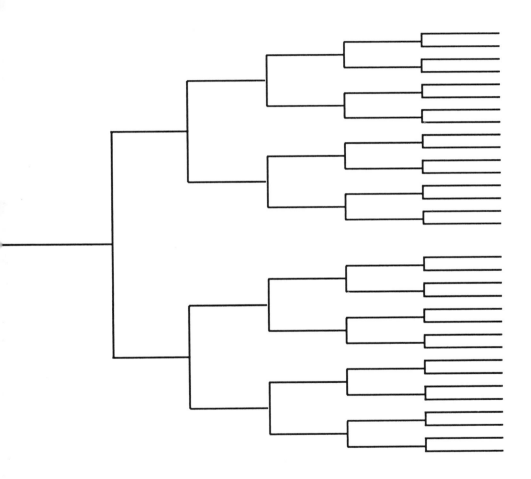